M000316617

YOU *Can* CHOOSE

© Copyright 2021- Beth McCoy

All rights reserved. Permission is granted to copy or reprint portions for any noncommercial use, except they may not be posted online without permission.

Some content taken from *50 Days of Heaven: Reflections That Bring Eternity to Light* by Randy Alcorn.© Copyright 2006. Used by permission of Tyndale House Publishers, a Division of Tyndale House Ministries. All rights reserved.

Unless otherwise indicated, all Scripture quotations are taken from the New American Standard Bible, *The Ryrie Study Bible* 1977.

Wyatt House books may be ordered through booksellers or by contacting:

Wyatt House Publishing
399 Lakeview Dr. W.
Mobile, Alabama   36695
www.wyattpublishing.com

Because of the dynamic nature of the Internet, any web address or links contained in this book may have changed since publication and may no longer be valid.

Cover design by: Mark Wyatt
Interior design by: Mark Wyatt

ISBN 13: 978-1-7345398-6-8

Printed in the United States of America

YOU *Can* CHOOSE *Joy*

by
BETH MCCOY

Wyatt House Publishing
Mobile, Alabama

I want to dedicate this book to my parents,
Joe and Lib Todd,
who lived an example of a life of steadfast faith
and to the glory of
our Lord Jesus Christ.

Foreword

For many years I have often thought, "I should write a book." In April, 2018, after speaking to a group of ladies in Vancouver, Washington, one of the women came up to me and told me she wished her mom could hear my son, Matt's, story. She asked if she could have a copy of my notes for her mom. I had gone so far off my notes that I knew they would not help. There was another woman standing there and she said, "It sounds like it's time for you to write a book." I laughed. Later, I felt the Lord laying the same thought on my heart. So finally, in December 2019, I started writing. I had always known that if I ever wrote a book about Matt that I would title it, "You *Can* Choose Joy".

Life events can sometimes steal our joy, and little did I know when I started that I would end up writing about joy in the middle of a pandemic and then social and political unrest (not to mention fires and hurricanes plaguing our nation). The timing hasn't been lost on me and the need to remember what I'm writing has been working in me and helping me, just as I hope it will help you.

If you are wondering where in the world you can find some joy through all this, I pray that Matt's story can help you. Parts of his life have been very difficult to re-live while writing, but in order for you to see how God has worked in our lives, you have to know the dark times, too. I am not a writer. I'm just a mom who wants to tell the story of what God has done in my son's life, and in doing this in Matt's life, He has also done it in mine. God is good. I pray you know the Joy of the Lord and that this book is a blessing in your life.

January 2, 1998 started as a gloriously beautiful morning in Vancouver, Washington. It was cold. The frost glistened like diamonds in the bright sunshine. Phil, our daughter Karen, her husband, Jimmy, and I had returned two days earlier from a Christmas trip in Georgia. Our son Matt and daughter-in-law Nicole had not been able to go with us. I had gotten up early to take advantage of the New Year's sales and Phil was in his office when he received the call that every parent dreads. It was a Clark County Deputy Sheriff.

"Reverend McCoy, this morning your son was involved in a car accident at the intersection of First Street and 164th Avenue."

Phil asked, "What happened?"

"He ran over black ice and slid into an oncoming truck."

"How is he?"

The officer answered, "He is being taken to Emanuel Hospital. He was alive when they left the scene."

Matt was twenty four years old.

Part One

"For this boy I prayed, and the Lord has given me my petition which I asked of Him. So I have dedicated him to the Lord..."

-I Samuel 1:27 and 28a *(NASB)*

"Thanks be to God for His Indescribable gift!"

I Corinthians 9:15 *(NASB)*

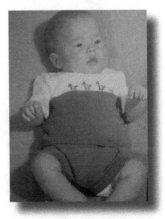

Matt at 3 months

Chapter One

Phillip Matthew McCoy was born in Newnan, Georgia on July 10, 1973 at 7:10 in the evening. My pregnancy had been uneventful except for some small issues in the first trimester. I just about worried myself to death about it until one day I decided to surrender him to God. (That was just the first time I did that over the last 47 years.) Labor and delivery were really very easy and lasted only about three hours. He was seven pounds and two ounces and twenty-two inches long; a perfect baby boy. He looked just like his daddy. The first time I held Matt, I felt like I had known him forever. I did not have that experience with Karen, our first born, but Phil did. He joined his sister, Karen, to make us a family of four. He was long and skinny and was born hungry. At that time, nursing was just becoming a more popular practice, but I did not nurse either of my children. Some people say we need to nurse our babies in order to bond with them. Well, if Matt and I had been any more bonded we would have had to be surgically separated!! And just for a little history, Richard Nixon was the president of the United States and Jimmy Carter was the Governor of Georgia. The four days we were in the hospital, the only thing on daytime TV was the Watergate Hearings.

When Matt was 13 days old, he began to run a fever. It took 3 days and as many doctor visits to discover that he had tonsillitis. This new Mama was beside herself and I felt so responsible because, maybe if I had been nursing him, he would have been protected from this sickness. After taking antibiotics for 10 days though, he was fine. I wondered then: is this a hint of things to come?

When Matt was six weeks old, he was dedicated to God at Cokes Chapel UMC by Rev. Charles Davis. His Christening dress was made in 1958 by Mrs. Opal Smith. (She was our neighbor and the church organist and was like a grandmother to me when I was growing up.) The dress had been worn by her granddaughters, Terry and Bonnie, and by Matt's aunt, Jennie, and his sister, Karen. The reason he was dedicated at such an early age was because he was so much larger than the girls. The dress was almost too small at six weeks.

He loved to eat everything; vegetables, meat, sweets, literally everything. He was a good talker and pretty easy to understand. He started walking around his first birthday and was a very happy little boy. Instead of working to make Matt smile for pictures, photographers had to work at calming him down and not smiling so big. He loved cars and trucks, dogs and cats, playing in the dirt, and riding his big wheel! When Matt was four, he got an award for being the happiest day camper! I just hope I can paint a picture for you about what a sweet and happy little boy Matt was. We had a pastor who told me that we should have named him "Isaac" because he laughed so much (Isaac means laughter.).   Karen and Matt got along pretty well, for siblings. She was a daddy's girl and Matt was a mama's boy. It seemed to work out pretty well at the time.

Matt really had a great imagination, sometimes it was too great! He was four when I was cleaning my mom's house and Matt came running in the house to show me his hand. He was very excited!

"Look, Mama, look what that squirrel did to me. He bit my hand!"

He had been outside playing in the dirt with his cars and trucks. I could not believe my ears so I said, "What?!"

He elaborated his story a little by saying he was playing in the dirt with his trucks when this squirrel jumped out of the tree and ran up to him and bit his hand. He did have two tiny marks on his hand, but a squirrel coming out of a tree? I'm not buying this one.

So he continued, "The squirrel is still out there. Come see!"

So I went outside where Matt's trucks were in the dirt and, sitting in the oak tree, there was a squirrel. On one of the low limbs that squirrel sat chattering at Matt like he was mad at him. I had never heard a sound from a squirrel before and I haven't heard one since. I cannot even describe the noise. Squirrels typically run from you, not toward you. So, of course, you know where my mind went next – RABIES!

For a few minutes I tried to scare the truth from Matt: "if a squirrel really bit you, you will have to have some shots or you could get really sick!" (I did not use the dead word, I thought that might be a little extreme for a little guy.) He stuck to his story. Even my daddy tried to get Matt to tell the truth. He was so sincere and serious! What else could I do but call the doctor? He was stymied; he had never heard of a squirrel biting someone so he called the CDC in Atlanta. It took about an hour to hear back from them. There had never been a case of rabies found in a rodent so we should not be concerned about it. I felt better, but I was not totally at peace. [I have read since then that rodents can indeed carry rabies, so I don't know what the real truth is.] Before I finished cleaning the house, he came up to me with this pitiful, sorry, "don't beat me" look on his face and said, "Mama, that squirrel didn't bite me. I cut my hand on my truck." Hallelujah! I was so relieved, but I thought I would need to scare him good so he would not pull a stunt like this again. I made him show me the truck and how he got scratched and then I told him, "Matt, you might have had to take shots for seven days! They give you those shots in your stomach and they hurt! And worse, you could die! Do not ever tell a story like that again! Mama and daddy need to be able to believe whatever you tell us." I think it worked. After that, if Matt tried to tell a lie, he had a "tell": his upper lip would do this weird thing. (He would get a small wrinkle between his lip and his nose, and his upper lip would quiver.) I think I scared him sufficiently, at least for a few years. It was a shake your head and just pray, "Lord, help" kind of experience.

The kids called my parents Grandmama and Granddaddy. Grandmama and my sister Jennie planned a trip to Gatlinburg, TN. They were taking Karen with them. Matt was probably four. When they came to get Karen, Matt begged to go. Mama did not want to take him because he would be so far from home and she thought he would get homesick. Well, he kept begging and promised that he would not want to come home and he would have a good time. They were somewhere in North Georgia when Matt said, "Grandmama, I think I shoulda oughta stayed at home." Then he got the word from her that she did not want to hear another word about it, and she didn't. Matt wanted to be home but he was agreeable and had a good time and didn't say another word about it. He was sure glad to see us when he did get home. But that became a family joke, "Grandmama, I think I shoulda oughta stayed at home."

One thing Matt loved to do was to "help" Granddaddy in his garden. As daddy would use his rototiller in the long rows Matt would follow; up and down the rows he would step where his granddaddy had stepped before him. It was the sweetest thing to watch, and he would do it for quite a while. I loved it and I know daddy did, too.

When Matt was almost four, we bought him a bunk bed. He was so excited! The bed arrived on a Saturday and, after it was set up, we discovered they had forgotten the ladder that went with them. No problem, they would deliver it the next Saturday. Now, the kids called Phil's parents Maxine and Hershel because when Karen was born Maxine did not think she was old enough to be called grandma (that's true, but if I could, I would put a smiley face here). Matt loved going to their house. So right after the bed was all set up, Matt went to Maxine and Hershel's and stayed several days. The ladder was delivered while he was there. He had not been home ten minutes before he jumped off the ladder and broke his left arm right below his shoulder. The break was not in the joint and the bone was not completely broken so he only had to keep his arm in a sling for several weeks. Thank the Lord! There were no complications and he healed up with only the annoyance of the sling. Sometime later, he jumped off the ladder onto his Rock 'em Sock 'em Robots game and cut the ball of his foot. He had to have stitches for that accident. Mysteriously, the ladder disappeared. No more accidents on the bed.

Matt was always a good talker. He spoke very plainly. From the beginning his words were clear and understandable – except for the letter "L" when it was the first letter in a word. For instance, love was "wuv" and like was "wike" and so on. It was so cute, really. He would say, "I wuv you Mama!" and I loved it. But he was approaching kindergarten so I thought we better fix this. I did not want the other kids to make fun of him, so I began to work with him. I would say, "Matt, say la, la, la, la..." and he would say, "la, la, la, la." We even made up songs and sang "Deck the Halls". He did great. Then we moved on to the word, love. He was able to repeat it perfectly. I thought this is great and it's been so easy!! So then I said, "say, I love you." And he said, "I wuv you, Mama." - another, Lord help, moment. But we didn't give up. By the time kindergarten started he was saying all of his "Ls" perfectly and I have to say that I missed his "I wuv yous" very much.

The First Methodist Church Kindergarten was Matt's first experience with school. He did very well until springtime. I guess he was just tired of it all. I still have some of his projects and his last one has several pages that are blank, and on one page his teacher wrote, "Matt just sits and says 'I can't'." (I'm afraid this was a hint of what school was going to be like for Matt.) I think she was pretty frustrated. I must admit that I was pretty frustrated that she wrote that on his paper. However, he did excel in Kindergarten Spanish. He really loved it.

Chapter Two

I think Matt was in the first grade when he asked Jesus into his heart. We had gone to a gospel music concert, and they had an altar call at the end of the service, and Matt went forward. The next day he told his teacher at school that he had asked Jesus into his heart. He was very excited about it, and so were we.

Grammar school went well. He managed to get through with good grades and good friends. His only broken bone was his shoulder from the bunk bed ladder incident. He went into the hospital when he was six to have his tonsils removed. Matt was a skinny kid. [He was wearing super slim jeans and they were still too big in the waist. He was asked to be the ring bearer in Phil's brother, Steve's, wedding. When he was measured for his tux, His measurements were: chest -20, waist-20, and hips-20. He still likes to tell people about those measurements!] Matt could eat a lot, but he was always skinny, until those tonsils were gone, then he began to gain some weight, and I was glad. It was so much easier to find pants that fit him.

Matt had cut his first two teeth when he was 3 months old, and he had seven teeth at 7 months old. His two front bottom teeth got loose and came out just like they were supposed to, but the four top front teeth did not. What made things even more complicated was that his bite was off and his bottom teeth were in front of his upper teeth. So our family dentist sent us to a pediatric dentist. The roots on his top four baby teeth did not dissolve and his right top permanent tooth was beginning to come out behind. After two and a half hours in the dentist chair, Matt's four teeth were pulled so his permanent teeth had a place to go. One tooth dropped down but the other did not. The x-rays showed an extra tooth that was blocking the new tooth. Another surgery to remove the extra tooth was successful, and after the dentist made a little cut in Matt's gum the tooth dropped down just like it was supposed to; however, it was sideways. Matt started wearing upper braces in the second grade. Maybe a year later at one of our regular appointments, his orthodontist said it appeared that Matt had grown another tooth and it would have to be removed. We were to come back in three months and, if the tooth was still there, then Matt would have to have more oral surgery. A couple of days before the appointment Matt was adamant, "nobody is going to cut on my mouth again!"

In God's timing, I had gone to the book store and purchased a little book mark that read, "God gives the best to those who leave the choice to Him." I had not put it away and it was lying on the kitchen table the morning of Matt's appointment. I had no idea he was reading it. He looked at me and said, "Mama, if God wants Dr. R to cut on me, he can cut on me." That was pretty smart for an eight year old. Well, we went to the appointment and the x-ray showed no extra tooth. Matt and I just looked at each other and on the way home, I told him, "Matt, Praise God, let's always remember this lesson that God taught us today." Surrender to Him and He will give us the best! He is the only one that really knows what is best. It may not be what we would choose, but God knows what is good and He will make it come to pass. He is good!

We enrolled Karen and Matt in a small Christian school, and they attended for two years. Karen did not like the school but Matt thrived. The discipline was pretty strict and Matt felt safe. Really the only thing good for Karen being there was that home didn't seem so strict anymore! Part of the curriculum was scripture memorization. We knew that was a good thing, but, after the first couple of days, Matt came home upset. He had to memorize Psalm 19 – the whole thing! So I said, "Don't worry, Matt, I will help you." So we started working on it together. Two days later, Matt had memorized the whole chapter and I was still working on the third verse! He did not need my help. (We did find out later that he only had to learn about half of it because he was in a lower grade.)

Because Matt and Karen attended private school, Spring break was always a different week than when their friends from public school were off so, Matt went to Maxine and Hershel's for five days. Maxine was an excellent cook. She also had MS so she was not able to do a lot of physical things with Matt. She loved on him by cooking. One night she fried chicken and fried four extra legs. Matt loved fried chicken and, after eating several legs, he asked for more. She told him that chicken only had six legs and they were all gone. He looked up at her and said, very seriously, "I bet that chicken sure could dance!" He had a great sense of humor, even then. He gained five pounds in five days and he loved every minute he spent with his grandparents. He would eat breakfast when he woke up, then he would have a snack, then he would eat lunch, then he would eat with Hershel when he came home for lunch, then he would eat supper and, finally, he would eat again with Hershel when he came home from work. Unless he needed a snack before bedtime... really! (He would've made a good Hobbit!) He did that two years in a row for spring break. I told him he couldn't go again unless he promised he would not eat so much! Little did I know that we would not be there for him to go the next year.

Chapter Three

In 1983, Phil surrendered his life to the Lordship of Jesus Christ. Then he and I felt the Lord's call to apply to World Gospel Mission to be missionaries at Peniel Mission, their Inner City ministry on the West Coast. Karen was thirteen and Matt was ten. Matt was a very compliant child and he did not mind the move. He never wanted to do anything to upset Mama and Daddy, especially Mama. Karen did not want to go and was very open about it. So, in August of 1983, we moved to Clinton, Mississippi where Phil attended Wesley Biblical Seminary in Jackson. First, we lived in a three bedroom apartment. It was very nice, but it was not a good experience for any of us. It was worse for Matt - he was picked on and bullied. His bicycle was even stolen from our porch. We attended Hinds Independent Methodist Church in Raymond, Mississippi. So when Mr. Gregory Wright invited us to put a trailer on his farm, we jumped at the chance. Karen and Matt were both happy there; we all were. Mr. Gregory and "Miss" Irene (Pap and Nana) treated our kids like their own grandchildren. Mr. Gregory's daughter, Janet and family lived in the big house behind us and his son, Dale and family lived in a house on the other side of the drive way. There were four boys that Matt played with on a farm with a pond. He was in true country boy heaven.

Matt decided he wanted to play baseball so he joined a little league team and practiced often. He was very excited when he received his baseball uniform. So, we loaded up and headed for Matt's first game. In one of the innings when Matt's team was at bat, we could not find him. Phil started walking around and found Matt playing with cars and trucks in the dirt with the little brother of one of his team mates. It turned out that Matt really just wanted a uniform. He was not ever going to be a baseball player.

While we were there, we adopted a dog named TC and Karen was given a kitten that grew into a cat named Ralph. Mississippi was a good experience for both of our children. We were there for almost two years. It was hard to say good-bye to a lot of good friends.

1985 found us moving back to Georgia with Phil driving a U-Haul and me driving our car. Matt and the dog, TC, rode with Phil, and Karen and the cat, Ralph were with me. We gave both the animals a sedative that the vet had given us because Ralph hated riding in the car so we thought that would be a good idea. Instead, Ralph went nuts! He clawed Karen! There was cat hair flying everywhere! He destroyed the beach towel that was covering him and after flying around Phil on the Interstate, we all pulled over. We got another towel, wrapped Ralph up like a mummy, and started on our way. As we got back on the road, the song playing on my cassette (yes, a cassette) was "His Grace is Greater." It's a good thing that it is true because I just wanted to throw Ralph out the window. But Karen loved that cat so I didn't seriously consider it. She held him in her lap for the eight hour trip to Georgia.

We lived with my parents for a year as we were on deputation: a time dedicated to raising prayer and financial support to go to the West Coast. By that time, we knew we were headed for Portland, Oregon. My parents were a great help. Daddy was retired so he was always there with the kids. Mama was an operating room nurse and she was still working. They supported us completely, but it was a difficult year for all of us. Usually, we traveled on the weekend, but, sometimes, we were gone during the week. Karen and Matt were in school and they went with us whenever they could and they were a great asset. They were friendly and well-behaved (they usually were in public). What more could we ask for? Deputation was so exciting – at first. After a while, the kids were not anxious to go and I thought if I have to get on I-20 again, I might scream. I never did scream (I just would go into a trance). We never made the kids go with us. So they were home with the Grands more and more.

Matt had some difficulties in school that year and I think I'll just leave it at that. Matt had, once again, repented and prayed for Jesus to live in his heart. Even then Matt was a good kid, but I think he might have been hiding a lot of negative feelings that he was experiencing.

The Lord blessed us on deputation and we were almost fully funded in that year. So in June of 1985, Phil, Karen, Matt, TC and I moved to Portland, OR. Phil was driving a Ryder Truck and I was driving our car. Usually, Matt and TC were with Phil, and Karen was with me. Karen had her learner's permit and would drive about an hour a day. (We did not know at the time that she probably was not a legal driver in many states.) [Ralph had gotten killed in the highway about a month before we moved, and Karen was heartbroken, but it was probably a good thing considering our previous moving experience with him.]

Matt attended Floyd Light Middle School in Portland, OR. It was a difficult year for him. Two things helped him adjust and enjoy most of the eighth grade; Miss Delight Knoepfle, and joining the chorus to be in the musical that year. Delight was a member of Oregon City Evangelical Church' (OCEC) and she was well-named. She was a true delight and her patience and attitude with Matt were a blessing to us that difficult year.

The youth pastor at OCEC was Tim Volkman, He had also attended Wesley Biblical in Jackson, MS. What a God thing! Both kids loved Tim and we knew when we moved that we would be attending Oregon City Evangel-ical Church. It was a point of light for the kids as we were moving away from everyone that we loved; Tim and his wife, Sue, would be there. And as God would have it, the church was a great blessing to all of us. Thankfully, we found a house to rent that was only 12 miles away from the church. Karen and Matt would not have cared if it had been 30 miles away.

In an attempt to ease the pain of moving, Phil had promised Matt that we would take him deep sea fish-ing in the Pacific Ocean. Matt had loved to fish since he could hold a fishing pole. He really was not particular-ly gifted at fishing, but he loved doing it. He wanted to fish whether he caught something or not, but he always wanted to catch some fish. More than once Phil and I found ourselves praying that the Lord would just put a fish on Matt's hook so we could go home. So in August, Phil, Matt and I went to Garibaldi, OR and went out on a fishing boat to catch some salmon in the ocean. (Kar-en did not want to go deep sea fishing.) It was freezing cold and rough getting out of Tillamook Bay very ear-ly in the morning. It was so foggy you couldn't see ten yards out from the boat. It was a little smoother out in the ocean, and after a while, we stopped to fish. Phil and Matt both were already seasick and taking Dramamine. There were only two other people on the boat with us, besides the captain and two shipmates.

The crew baited the hooks and put the poles in a holder. They would yell "fish on!!" and someone would grab the pole and start reeling in the fish. Well, the other people got the first two poles. At the next "fish on" I told Matt to grab the pole. He really didn't feel very good so he did not want to. Well, I made him take up the pole and he had a great time. All he needed was something other than his stomach to concentrate on. We were limited to two silver salmon each and we all caught our limit - each one weighing around ten pounds. Then the crew fished for their limit. By that time the sun had come out and it wasn't as cold. Phil and Matt slept off the Dramamine all the way back to Garibaldi. The only other lady on the boat had caught a 65 pound Chinook. That was a huge fish! Because I had a Polaroid camera with me, the Captain offered me a deal to clean and package our six fish for some pictures of the catch of the day. That was one of the better deals I have made in my life. Matt did have a great time, but we never went deep sea fishing again. [We didn't even get to eat all the junk food we took or use the sun screen. We were not fishing in the Gulf of Mexico; we were in the Pacific Ocean – big difference. The water was very rough and it was cloudy and cold.]

Matt was a late bloomer. He didn't play with cars and trucks anymore, but he loved GI JOE. Matt loved everything military. He read about weapons and ammunition and had absolutely no trouble remembering everything he read. As a matter of fact, Matt pretty much remembered anything he read. I remember the year before we moved to Mississippi, Grandmama and Jennie took Karen and Matt on a trip out west. They went to the Grand Canyon, Brice, Zion, Salt Lake City, Yellowstone, and the Dinosaur Monument. Matt did not ever get home sick, he had pretty much grown out of that, but he knew something about almost everything they saw and wasn't bashful about sharing his knowledge. He almost drove them crazy.

Phil and I were busy learning about the mission and we were not completely funded so we were still on deputation. Phil was working as the Volunteer director of Portland Peniel Mission and I was his assistant. By the end of September of 1986 we were funded and were released to officially work on the Peniel Field.

Two times a year we went to Sacramento, California for business meetings and spiritual renewal with the Peniel Field. Sometimes Karen and Matt went with us. When Matt was about 14 we attended and Matt felt the Lord calling him to be a missionary and work with children. We were so excited. That same year Christmas was on a Sunday, and if I remember this correctly, the pastor asked if anyone wanted to share anything about what the Lord had done for them in the last year. What I remember well is that Matt stood up and again said that he felt the Lord's call to be a missionary! That was a good thing! We prayed for both of our children that God would use them and they would be obedient to His calling! We thought, Praise the Lord, Matt was headed in the right direction! Now we would just wait and see what Karen would do. We had no idea what road the Lord was going to lead us down. And it is a good thing that we cannot look into and know the future. It is enough that God can and does.

Chapter Four

In 1987, Karen was a senior and Matt entered David Douglas High School. I don't think they saw much of each other at school and they were not really close. He didn't have any serious girl friends in high school, but there were several girls that were his friend.

In the 9th grade, Matt just about quit growing. His shoe size didn't change for 18 months. He gained a lot of weight and I think he was pretty depressed. He absolutely hated school. Matt got an F in PE, and that was not acceptable! We really had no idea what was going on with him. He was struggling in all his classes which was so frustrating because he really was so smart. After a conference with his teacher, we found out that he wouldn't change clothes in front of the other boys. He had always been modest, but he had to change clothes. What we did not know was that the boys were making fun of him because he was a late bloomer. The happy little boy we had known was gone. He even tried choir again, but he and the director did not hit it off. He seemed to be done growing. I started to pray that Matt would grow, and at least get taller than I was. He hit a wall at 5'8" and I was 5'9".

During that time, Matt was generally not feeling well. He was studying diabetes in school and he kept telling me that he had diabetes. I kept saying, "No, you don't!" Well, finally I took him to the doctor and his blood sugar was somewhere around 350. I felt like the scum of the earth mother! My negligence could have killed my son! I had to take him back the next morning to have blood drawn for a fasting blood test. When the report came back his numbers were perfectly normal. I gave the Lord credit for healing him and maybe He did, but sometime later Matt told me he had a large Coke and a large Snickers bar before the first test. But, as I observed him, it did seem that his body really didn't process a lot of sugar well. So, I limited his sugar intake the best I could.

As you can imagine we did not make a lot of money as missionaries, especially for the cost of living on the West Coast. I would carefully plan our meals and sometimes they were pitiful. I would open the refrigerator, thinking I had leftovers to have for supper, only to find that Matt had eaten them for an afternoon snack. It happened more than once. I can't remember what I threatened him with, but it must have been good. He never did it again. I did try to provide snacks for him because he was a teenage boy, he was always hungry.

The tenth grade did not start off any better. There was no in-between for his teachers, they either couldn't stand him or they loved him. He got in trouble in American History when he answered the teacher with an answer only a southerner would appreciate. The question was: "What other name was used for the American Civil War?" Now, I don't know if Matt volunteered his answer or the teacher called on him, but he replied, "The War of Northern Aggression." It was not well received, even though the teacher did not specify it had to be a northern name. I can't remember what that cost Matt, but he thought it was worth it.

Around Matt's 15th birthday my brother, John, came to visit and we went camping at Yosemite National Park in California. Matt had a crush on his sister's friend, Jody. She was a beautiful girl and Matt would almost melt if you just said her name. It was pretty funny. Jody never knew and Karen, well, being his sister, knew Matt was out of his league as she was three years older than Matt. His dad and his Uncle Johnny teased him mercilessly about her. He counted his underarm hairs – all six of them - every night. He was then asked, "How many do you have tonight, Matt?" He certainly gave his daddy and uncle plenty of ammunition to tease him on that trip.

Karen graduated and went to college for two years in Canada. Matt missed her greatly, but after a little while, I think he did enjoy being the only kid at home. At the time I came up with a brilliant plan to divide up my time at the mission so I could be home more but, actually, the new schedule accomplished the opposite. Matt ended up being home by himself even more. I was really concerned about him during this time. The new schedule did not last long. Matt still had some time by himself at home, there was no way to avoid it, but the old schedule was a better one. He went through some depression and I prayed for him a lot. But he was such a good son, obedient and respectful. He wasn't obsessed with having a girlfriend like most his age. Although, he did have girls calling him since the 8th grade. His main problem was with school. Looking back, I just think Matt was terrified most of the time. It hurt me when I finally realized that – a little too late.

I have failed to mention that Matt is a huge Georgia Bulldog fan! He owned a red Georgia Jacket and, at the time, Nike sold solid red athletic shoes. He had gotten a job at one of the shoe stores at Mall 205 in Portland. He could walk or ride his bike to work, which was nice. He got a very good discount. Matt had saved his money and, with his discount, he bought a new pair. Now, at the time gang activity was growing in Portland. There were two main gangs; the Crips and the Bloods. The Crips wore blue and the Bloods wore red. People were warned: Do not wear blue or red in downtown Portland, if you do you are going to make yourself a target! Matt wore his Georgia outfit to school one day and it wasn't a good idea. He was told not to wear red, even if it was your favorite college team's colors! I'm not certain, but I think he may have worn some red sweat pants too. He still loves red and the Georgia Bulldogs and, happily we don't have to even think about the Bloods any more. Portland was proving to not be an easy place for this southern boy.

Matt finally began to grow and shot up and slimmed down. His feet, that had not grown in over a year, changed three sizes in 6 weeks. He was fitting his shoes himself and I asked him if he was doing it correctly. He assured me he had a coworker check his new shoes. He was growing so fast I thought his feet should hurt but he said he had no pain. Matt grew three to four inches during the summer between his junior and senior year. What a shock it must have been for all the bullies that had picked on him for three years. Thankfully, Matt never retaliated (that I know of). He was just happy to have blossomed, better late than never.

Around this time, Phil and Matt seemed to get a little competitive toward each other. It might start with who was the tallest or strongest and they both were tall and strong, but it would usually end with Matt smacking his daddy's upper arm with his fist and then Phil smacking him back. You may not be surprised to know that I didn't like it at all! Somebody was going to get mad or hurt or both. So one day their little game was going on and I was yelling at them to stop. In the middle of it all the Lord spoke to me - this thought went through my mind like a streak of lightning; "He will be all I want him to be if you don't give up." I will not ever forget it. I didn't understand it at the time, but that message from God was one day going to be a lifeline for me.

Matt has been patriotic all of his life. If you talk to him now about World War II, he will tell you that his granddaddy was at Pearl Harbor on December 7th. He will even tell me "My granddaddy was there when Pearl Harbor was bombed!" I always answer, "I know, Matt". He's very proud of that, and so am I. I remember in 1978 - Matt was five -when the hostages were taken in Iran. Matt watched the News and when he saw the pictures of the hostages and that the Iranians were burning the American Flag, he was ready to go fight! Then, in 1991, Matt was a senior at David Douglas High School in Portland, OR when America went to war with Iraq. It was called Operation Desert Storm and Matt helped organize a rally during lunch for the students to support the troops. So to support the troops and my son, I drove down to David Douglas to be part of the rally. I was turned back by a school employee and informed that the students did not have permission to hold a rally and there would not be one. I thought uh-oh, but as far as I ever knew Matt did not get in trouble for trying to have a rally to support our troops and I was very proud of him for wanting to.

Matt had a very good eye for pictures, especially pictures of nature. His Grandmama gave him her 35mm camera and he got a tripod for Christmas one year. I have wonderful pictures of Half Dome in Yosemite, of waterfalls in north Georgia, Mt. St. Helens, fireworks and waterfalls in the Columbia River Gorge. He really was good and he enjoyed it. The only problem is that you can't rush genius. It took Matt a long time to get the picture he wanted. They say that is the mark of a good photographer: patience. That was one gift Matt had – patience – at least when he was fishing or taking a picture.

Matt got a job after school and Saturdays at Chick-Fil-A at Clackamas Town Center when he was a senior. I believe it was the only Chick-Fil-A in Portland. (He had to work to pay for his insurance on his car. He could drive to Oregon City for youth events and that was a huge help to us.) It was a really good place to work; he didn't have to work on Sunday, his boss was a really nice guy and the pay was pretty good. The bad part about working was the hours. The mall closed at ten. Matt was working some nights until ten and then getting up to go to school the next morning. Christmas was absolutely the worst time. He would get home at eleven, or sometimes later, on school nights. One night I was already in bed reading when Matt came in to say goodnight. I looked up to tell him goodnight and jumped straight up out of that bed in a second! Matt's face was scraped and he had scrapes on his hands and arms. Someone had jumped him in the parking lot when he was walking back to his car. By this time, Matt was at least 6'1". Evidently, being tall and strong was not enough to protect him. We never knew who did it and he was really fine, but the event had a lasting impact on his life.

Matt barely graduated in June 1991 and was accepted at Toccoa Falls College in North Georgia. I flew to Georgia while Phil and Matt drove across the country in his Dodge colt with Matt's belongings and TC the dog. It was a really good trip for them. He stayed that summer with my parents, and worked at the Winn Dixie in Newnan. I need to reiterate before I move on and say that even though Matt really struggled in high school, he was still a good kid. He was a hard worker and would do anything to help somebody. All the older folks in the neighborhood loved him. He was friendly and respectful. (The summers before both his sophomore and junior years, he stayed for a week with friends in Beaver, OR to help their church with Vacation Bible School (VBS). They lived on a small farm on the Little Nestucca River and Matt loved it. He loved helping with the children in VBS and all of the adults bragged about how respectful, helpful and willing he was with whatever they asked him to do. He was good at working with kids. The summer before his senior year, when he grew so much, he got a job doing landscaping. His boss, Lance, was very encouraging with how much he enjoyed having Matt work for him because he was respectful and a very hard worker. He would've been the perfect son, if he had not had to go to school.) He only stayed in college one quarter. So Phil flew to Atlanta and he and Matt drove once again across country in the Dodge Colt- this time to Vancouver, WA. (TC the dog stayed in Georgia where he enjoyed his retirement in the South.) Let's just say, sometimes, you just can't go back home.

Childhood had been a wide spectrum of emotions and events for Matt. He had excelled and struggled. He had been happy and sad. We had indeed moved a lot, but always with a purpose to follow God and he had the stability of parents that loved each other. His grandparents and aunts and uncles, and cousins loved us all wherever we were, and God provided people to fill those gaps wherever we lived. He had played in the surf of the Atlantic Ocean, the Gulf of Mexico and the Pacific Ocean. He had been to Roosevelt's Little White House in Warm Springs, GA and Lincoln's birthplace in Hodgenville, KY. He had hiked on Mt. St. Helens, in Yosemite, and played in the snow on Mt. Hood. He rode the rides at Disneyworld and Disneyland. He had flown and driven across the country numerous times. He had a lot of great experiences, but only the Lord knew what the future would be for him.

Chapter Five

He got home from college and enlisted in the Air Force. By this time, Phil and I had left the mission and were assigned to East Vancouver Community Church in Vancouver, WA, and Matt had totally forgotten his call to be a missionary. I brought it up only one time and he informed me that he had never said he wanted to be a missionary and never felt that God had called him to be one. Matt loved being an MK but he really disliked being a preacher's kid. He would say he was an MPK – a Miserable Preacher's Kid. He felt like he was constantly being watched and judged. He really wasn't, everybody at EVCC loved him but -when you are running from God you have to blame your guilt on somebody! And his dad and I prayed.

Matt joined the Air Force in 1992 and his enlistment lasted for about a month. This time-line may be a little spotty because I don't remember all the details and Matt is not clear on them either. But, in his first week at Lackland Air Force base in San Antonio, Texas, Matt slipped in the shower and injured his knee. His knee cap would slip out of alignment and cause terrible pain. It was a pre-existing condition; so, before they would accept him, he had to go to the doctor and get a waiver for this pre-existing condition. Since it was pre-existing, he was sent home and had to have surgery to repair his knee. He was formally separated from the Air Force in 1992. He was very disappointed.

It took weeks to finalize his separation and, when he got home from Texas, after recuperating from surgery, Matt decided he wanted to be a paramedic. He went to school and passed his first level. He did very well: and had no problem studying something he wanted to study. He began to ride along with the EMTs in North Portland. At one of their calls, the ambulance he was in was shot at – which didn't seem to bother Matt. It freaked me out! Then, one night, they were called and a two year old baby was involved. I don't remember the details, but the baby died in Matt's arms. He quit the emergency business and said his heart couldn't take it.

At the time, Matt was living at home and, he was accident prone. He has scars on both his arms from working on his Dodge Colt. Karen teased him about being on a first name basis with the ER nurses at the hospital, and not from his brief training as an EMT. At some point during this time, Matt decided he was going to buy a motorcycle. Now you have to have a little history to try to understand my reaction. My mom was a nurse and had seen many motorcycle accident victims in her life. She shared those stories with us over the years. My daddy's nephew was on a motorcycle in Atlanta when he was hit by a car because the driver just did not see him. He was paralyzed from the waist down. So, between my cousin and my mother's stories, I was totally against my accident-prone son riding around on a motorcycle. (To this day, I have never been on one and do not plan to ever be on one!) Anyway, to be brutally honest, these words came out of my mouth to my son: "Well, if you have an accident and end up in a nursing home, don't expect me to come see you every day!" His daddy agreed. He did not buy the motorcycle; but, we should be very careful what words come out of our mouths, because they can come back to haunt us.

In July of 1992, Karen got engaged to Jimmy Robinson who she had been dating since High School. The wedding date was set for August 1993. Around January 1993, Karen moved home to prepare for the wedding, to learn to cook and to save money. Let's just say, we prepared and had a beautiful wedding. Matt got really fed up with the wedding plans, and having his sister at home, so he moved out sometime that spring. He moved into an apartment with his friend, Wes. That experience had him saying he would never get married.

Chapter Six

Matt's next endeavor at employment was as a pharmacy Tech Assistant at Hi-School Pharmacy. He did very well and the company was willing to help him go to Pharmacy Tech School but, Matt didn't get along with the Pharmacist there, and he quit that job. While he was there, he was chosen to be in a TV commercial. He was tall and handsome and he looked really good on TV. One day a young lady, Nicole, came into the store and looked up at him and said, "Hey, I saw you on TV!" They dated a couple of weeks, became engaged and were married about nine months later. On their wedding day he had been twenty one for only twenty days. As soon as he turned 21 he got a permit and purchased a hand gun. He took it almost everywhere he went. Even though he had grown to 6 feet 4 inches, on the inside, he was still afraid because of all the years of bullying. He was determined no one would bully him again.

This part of the story is difficult for me and I wish I could just forget it, but you have to hear it to understand the depth of what God has done in him and through him and for him and for us. Just before their wedding, Matt had defended Nicole by tazing a girl who was verbally, and Matt felt was about to physically, attack her. It's a long story, but he ended up pleading guilty to a misdemeanor for it.

Over the next three and a half years, Matt worked at Vancouver Clinic in their billing department, a carpet cleaning company, Sealy Mattress Co., and a local dairy. While he was working for the carpet cleaning company he was rear-ended on the I-5 Bridge and taken, by ambulance, to the ER in Vancouver. He was checked out and released. The hospital had called us and, of course, we went there right away not knowing the extent of his injuries. We were very relieved when we arrived to find him sitting up in bed talking. While we were there, we met our "other son". A friend and neighbor of Matt's had lied to the nurse so he could go back and see him. He also worked with Matt at Sealy Mattress Co. They lived in at least four different apartment complexes over those three and a half years, and his car was broken into and trashed at one of them. It seemed something was always happening to him.

The last apartment complex was a very bad place to live - a lot of crime and drugs. In January, 1997, late one night their neighbors were being very loud and rowdy. Matt and Nicole had to get up and go to work the next morning. So, Matt got dressed and grabbed his hand gun and went down to the neighbors to get them to be quiet. I only know Matt's side of the story, but, he was by himself and, at some point, he felt very threatened so he showed the man the gun. There was a tussle and the gun went off. No one was hurt, thank God, but there were several people in the apartment and at least one child. Matt yelled for his friend ("our son") who had run to see what was happening, to call the police. The police came and they arrested Matt, and he spent three days in jail. It was a nightmare. My sweet son, the one who wanted to be a missionary and minister to children, was in jail and being accused of trying to shoot someone. After three days, Phil, I and Nicole went to the courthouse for his arraignment. It is quite a shock to your system to see your son dressed in orange with his hands and feet in chains. He was charged with reckless endangerment with a fire arm. He pled not guilty. The judge was not going to allow Matt to move back to that apartment, so he asked Matt if he had someone he could stay with. Matt looked back at us and said, "I can live with my parents." Nicole just looked at me and I patted her on the knee and smiled.

They did live with us, for about six months. Matt's friend had told their boss at Sealy that Matt was absent because his grandmother died. (Another lie) When Matt returned to work, he was fired for missing too many days. I don't remember how long he was unemployed, but we treated them the same as we did Karen and Jimmy. Karen and Jimmy had bought a house in Vancouver so they offered to store Matt's furniture while they were living with us. Matt and Nicole were in church most Sundays (I loved having all my family together in church) and were part of one of our church's small group Bible studies. We would all have Sunday lunch together. We tried to support them the best we could. I remember Matt telling me he just did not know what to do. I felt Matt had been, like Jonah, in the belly of the fish for the three days he was in jail and I told him so. Then I asked what was God saying to him? He did not know what God wanted them to do. I told him that when we don't know what to do, we do what we already know we are supposed to do. We read our Bible. We pray. We tithe. We spend time with other believers. We go to church and we trust God to lead us. Then we follow where He leads. I thought their time with us went as well as it could have, but, in another respect, it was an extremely difficult time. The uncertainty of his future was a nightmare. Where was my son going to spend the next years of his life? The DA of Clark County at that time was very anti-gun and he was going to make an example of him and Matt had no advocate - no one to testify for him. So, finally, in June, 1997, Matt plead guilty of reckless endangerment with a fire arm. My son was a felon. Thankfully, he did not have to serve any time. He had to go to anger management classes and had to see a parole officer regularly. He also had to serve weekly community service as roadside trash pick-up, and pay a monthly fine.

They eventually moved into another apartment a couple of miles away from us. Matt had gotten a job at a local dairy taking care of heifers and new mamas with their calves. He really loved his new job. In October, everyone was at our house for Sunday lunch when Matt and Nicole got into a terrible argument with Karen and Jimmy. I do not need to go into details, but we did not see much of Matt over the next few months. They didn't come to church very often and did not come to lunch on Sundays. That was their choice, not ours. I began to pray a different prayer, and I was desperate. I prayed, "Lord, do whatever it takes; bring Matt back to Yourself and to us." I never dreamed how God would answer that prayer.

Matt at 4 years old

Voted Happiest Day Camper!

How he earned his nickname of "Matt the Hat"

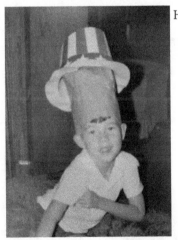

Little League Matt

Matt and Karen at his uncle's wedding. Matt's measurements were 20-20-20.

Matt's 3rd grade picture

Taking pictures at Yosemite

Matt's Dodge Colt

Matt's Senior Portrait

Part Two

He said, "This sickness is not unto death, but
for the glory of God, that the Son of God
may be glorified by it."

John 11:4

Jesus said to her, "Did I not say to you, if
you believe, you will see the glory God?"

John 11:40

"I will tell of Your name to my brethren;
in the midst of the assembly I will praise
You."

Psalm 22:22

Chapter Seven

December 7, 1941 changed the world. September 11, 2001 is a date that changed America. On January 2, 1998 the McCoy family was changed forever. It was a beautiful morning. Phil and I had returned from Georgia on New Year's Eve and Matt and Nicole had spent most of New Year's afternoon with us. It was a really good visit. We even discussed some of the issues they had discussed in their small group. (I do not remember if they were still attending at the time or not.) I woke up very early and headed for the Mall. I had received a gift certificate and I was going to take advantage of the sales. I had a great time and found several great deals and I went to Phil's office to show him my loot.

I arrived and Phil's car was gone, but Nicole's car was there. I won't go into all the details, but Phil's secretary, Gwen, made me sit down and call Karen. (My crazy thought was that this is not how Karen would tell me that she is having a baby!) Anyway, I called and she told me Matt had been in an accident and had been taken to Emanuel Hospital in Portland. I knew it was serious, Emanuel was a trauma center, but the name of the hospital was not lost on me - Emanuel, I also knew that God was with us.

Karen and Jimmy were waiting at home for me so they could take me to the hospital. Apparently, everyone had been looking for me for over an hour. (Phil had a cell phone, but I did not.) They had no new report on Matt. We found Phil and Nicole in the trauma unit waiting room. They had no news. They had not even seen Matt. There weren't many people in the waiting room and there was no volunteer to give us information, probably because it was a holiday weekend. So we sat down to wait. I thank God for Karen and Jimmy and their strength and presence that day. As we waited for news, I started to feel a little nauseous. I needed food. All I could say was, "I think I need something to eat" and Jimmy disappeared. He returned with bagels and that was just what I needed. Over the next few days, I don't know how many times he went to Roake's (his restaurant) and brought back hamburgers and chicken sandwiches.

Soon people began to come; Our good church friends, Rich and Nancy Lindsley and Gail Knoepfle, Rob Robinson (Jimmy's dad), friends from OCEC, Ron, Leona and Jeremy Harlin, Matt and Nikki Sumner and others, many others. (Jeremy and Matt were Matt's best friends from high school.) I called my parents so they could be praying.

Matt's accident occurred about 7:30 a.m. He was driving to work and drove over black ice in the intersection of 164th Ave. and First St. in Vancouver, WA. He was driving an old Volkswagen (it was a year older than he was) and he lost control. He crossed the center line spinning into the path of a pick-up truck and crashed into the truck on Matt's passenger side. (Miracle: it was not his side) The police officer was at the scene immediately. He did not witness it, but he was close by when it happened. The road was closed for hours. They had to investigate everything and talk to witnesses in case there was a fatality. We did get the call about two weeks later that Matt would not be charged for the accident- the cause was black ice. That was one thing I had not been concerned about. It had not crossed my mind that Matt could be charged for the accident. He had $25,000 of liability insurance. That was it. The driver of the truck was a nice young man named Scott; he called two times to check on Matt. He is the one that told us that Matt was wearing his seat belt and that he (Scott) had almost stopped before Matt hit him. He tried to get out of his way, but could not. Thankfully, there was no damage to Scott or his truck.

Finally, close to five hours after the accident, a nurse came out and told us about Matt's injuries. His right side was damaged; all of his ribs including his collar bone were broken, his spleen was torn and his liver was torn. Thankfully, there was no spinal injury! Part of his right lung had collapsed and his kidneys were affected. They were watching the spleen and the liver to see if they would seal up by themselves. He had little tears that they called shearing in his brain, both hemispheres. He was in a drug induced coma to give his brain time to heal and he was on a respirator. She could not answer our questions, but a doctor would be out soon to talk to us. Well, a doctor did come out and told us that Matt's internal injuries were under control. He told us the paramedics that brought Matt told him that Matt was the passenger of the car and he was not wearing his seatbelt. Both of those statements were strange and incorrect. Matt was driving his car, always wore his seatbelt and he was the only person in the car.

Well, that was all good news. His spleen and liver were okay. He made the little tears in the brain sound almost superficial - like we had nothing to worry about. So, I made some phone calls to share the news. Then, Dr. Irwin, the neurologist came out. All of Matt's injuries were minor compared to the brain injuries. She explained that all the different sections of the brain have different densities and they all weigh different amounts. So when you come to a very sudden stop like Matt did, those sections slam around in your skull at different speeds and they rip apart. When I asked when he would wake up, she said "I don't know if he will wake up". I was already in a fog, but when I heard those words, what I call my God Bubble, was complete. Some people might call it shock. I prefer to believe it is God – His Presence and His Peace. I could only pray one thing. My Lord and my God, Your will be done! I heard everything the doctors and nurses said, but it couldn't hurt me. I was totally aware. The news was upsetting, but I was totally protected. My sister called after this report and when I shared with her, she said, "Mama and I will be there tomorrow!"

At that time, the visiting hours at Emmanuel for the trauma center were ten minutes every two hours, two visitors at a time. Finally, they came and said that we could see Matt. Nicole wanted her mom to go with her, so it looked like I wouldn't get to see him, but the nurse took pity and let the three of us go in. They were behind me and she was being helped by her mom and the nurse. I saw Matt first. He looked like he was asleep. I turned around and told them, "Don't worry, he looks really good, like he is sleeping." The only bruise we could see was his right shoulder. There was a little bit of blood on his ear, but that was from a cut on his ear. The respirator tube was in his mouth and there were tubes everywhere. To measure the pressure they had put a monitor in his brain. It was toward the front of his head and it was wrapped with white tape and really looked like the tin hat the Tin Man wore in the Wizard of Oz. He was totally non-responsive.

At eight o'clock we went in for our last visit. The nurse was very busy connecting tubes and putting up bags of fluid and when we asked her what she was doing, she said I'm just getting ready for when his brain starts to swell. The nurses encouraged us to go home and rest so Phil and I went home for the night and Nicole and

Karen and Jimmy stayed with Rob and Linda, Jimmy's parents. They lived only a few minutes away from the hospital.

Matt held his own the first night. The next morning he was moving a little, but not responsive to us or the nurses. Mama and Jennie flew in from Atlanta and got to the hospital in time for the noon visit. Mama took Matt's hand and told him, "Matt, I think you shoulda oughta stayed at home yesterday morning!" We all smiled, except for Matt.

He was monitored for everything: pressure on his brain, BP, pulse, respiration, oxygen levels and probably more. There was a male nurse on duty that day and he told us, "He knows you're here." And we asked him, "How do you know?" He explained all the numbers on the monitors and told us that Matt's blood pressure and pulse go up when he hears our voices. We were encouraged, but all I wanted to do was crawl up in the bed and hold him. We could touch him, but there was never a response - just the numbers on the monitors. All of us were saying, "Matt, open your eyes! Please, open your eyes and look at us!" The fact that God was in control was really starting to sink in. Honestly, I knew He was answering my prayer: God was doing whatever it took to bring Matt back to the path God desired for him.

It was a long second day and we left to go home. Nicole went with Rob and Linda, Jennie went with Jimmy and Karen, and Mama came to our house. We weren't sure what we would do the next morning. Duane Koehler, our youth pastor, was going to preach for Phil. We were taking things day by day.

Chapter Eight

I woke up early and read my Bible and I knew only one thing. I needed to be in church. Then I made some phone calls to some of our pastors and asked them to have their churches pray for Matt. Randy Butler, Randy Meyers, Chris Nielson, Ron Johnson, Mark Purkey, Jim Trosen and Jimmy Knodel and their churches were among the first that were called on to pray. So we went to see Matt and then went to church. I was supposed to be leading the music that morning, but my friend Linda Melcher took over for me. We ended up on the second row and I cried all through the service. There were lots of tears and lots of love around the altar that morning.

We went back to the hospital after church. Matt had two drain tubes in his right lung. His gut was not working at all, but his kidneys were functioning some. A lot of people came to the waiting room that day. In one of our visits, we agitated Matt by trying to get him to wake up. The nurse showed us the monitor and the numbers were sky high, so we hushed. Then I asked if I could sing to him. I started to sing about Jesus; hymns and choruses

- and the numbers started going down. It was amazing.

At the 8 o'clock visitation the nurse asked us to stay because the doctor wanted to talk to us. Dr. Irwin told us that Matt's condition was being upgraded and he had been taken off the critical list. We were encouraged - for a second. What that meant was that they did not expect Matt to die. (Miracle: Matt's brain had not swollen like they expected it to!) She was still saying that she did not know if he would ever wake up. They also wanted to talk about the plan for Matt and they were looking for a Nursing facility for him. I didn't say anything, but this was my thought: "not my son, my son will either go to heaven or come home. There will be no nursing home for him." I'm so glad I did not say that out loud.

Of course, everyone was waiting for us and we shared the good news and the bad. We were seated in a kind-of circle and people were talking. I was sitting next to Jimmy's dad, Rob Robinson and, suddenly, I felt like warm oil was being poured over me - an anointing that was releasing peace all through me and my heart was strangely lifted. I turned to Rob and Linda and I told them and anyone else that was listening that very thing: "I feel my heart strangely lifted." (Another miracle) I wrote this in my journal,

"I know now that Matt will be healed. I don't know how or when or where he'll be when he wakes up and it is all right that he is not awake yet."

At one point, the nurse rubbed her thumb on the sole of Matt's foot and he opened his eyes, but there was nothing there; no light, no awareness, nothing. I decided I would happily wait on the Lord and let Him open Matt's eyes when He wanted to. I did not want to see that emptiness again.

There were a few people that had been with us that whole weekend and many who had been there for several hours. Our good friends, Rich and Nancy, were teachers and they had to go back to work the following day, but they had been there with us since Friday morning. Rob and Linda had also been there. Linda had to go back to work the next day too but Rob, who was a pastor, continued to come. I feel I need to say this: they were the perfect friends for us at that time. They didn't feel the need to share any wisdom, and they didn't feel the need to ask a lot of questions. They didn't even quote scripture. They just felt the need to be there, and they were. At the end of day three Matt's hospital bill was nearly $100,000.00. He only had $25,000 through his car insurance.

On day four, Matt had pneumonia which was not unusual for the type of accident he had. They put a dual feeding tube through his belly instead of going down his throat. One tube stopped in his stomach and the other went to his small intestine for the strong meds he was given. He had a nasal tube to remove food from his stomach because his intestines were still not working. I rubbed his head that day and he did not like it! I thought that maybe I would have to pester him back to us.

We felt the prayers of God's people so deeply. He was on prayer chains and church prayer lines that reached around the world. We were receiving cards, letters and phone calls from people we did not even know. I didn't worry that I could hardly pray; people were doing it for me. All I could pray was, "Your will be done." Evangeline and Burton Schwartz, WGM's representatives in the Northwest, asked me how they could pray for me. I replied that it would really help if I could sleep more than three or four hours a night. (Miracle: that night I slept seven hours.)

The next day, Tuesday, Mama and Jennie went home to Georgia. It was so good that they had been with us. Jennie understood all the technical stuff and could explain things to us that we did not understand. (She told me later that she came out to protect me, but didn't feel like she needed to after she arrived. She did not elaborate on why she didn't need to.) Actually, they were very entertaining and Mama, was my Mama. Just her presence was enough to help me, but it was time for them to go home. On that day they did a tracheotomy to get the tubes out of his mouth (he still had the NG tube in his nose to empty his stomach). It stressed Matt out pretty good, but he still looked so much better without all those tubes in his mouth.

I had asked Anne, Matt's nurse; if some pastors could come in and pray for Matt. She was in total agreement. As I remember them, her exact words were, "By all means that is the only thing that is really going to help him." (Another miracle) At four o'clock that day, Nicole,

Karen, Phil, Vic Slaughter, Rob Robinson, and I entered Matt's room. Percy McKnight, Dave Wildermuth, Jim Trosen, Bill Vermillion, and Jimmy Knodel, all pastors, were praying in the waiting room. He was anointed with oil and we prayed for his healing. He gave no immediate response at all. However, that day they did start weaning him from the respirator. He was initiating each breath, but still needed help – a step in the right direction. As we left for the day, the nurse encouraged us and told us to keep praying. She had seen it make all the difference.

Day 6: I started taking my Bible in the room with me and reading Matt a different verse every morning. I did not write down what my first verse was, but "I can do all things through Him who strengthens me." (Philippians 4:13) was read frequently, and they were always verses I found as I was reading or studying.

The residents were always coming in on their rounds and Dr. Paduch was the chief resident. On this day he came in with two others while we were there for our visit. Nurse Anne looked at me and said for me to go ahead and sing to him even though the doctors were there! So I did. (That part was too funny not to share.) Then, Dr. Paduch talked to us and said there were positive things going on. Matt responded to pain, he never got as bad as they expected, he was not doing destructive things (thrashing or pulling on his tubes), his heart was healthy and his kidneys were working. He warned us one more time - this is just going to be a long process. Wait! Wait! Wait! Waiting is hard! Waiting on the Lord is not always easy either, but it sure is easier than just waiting! God was working in Matt and maybe even through him.

Phil had a dream that night: there was an angel working on Matt's head putting everything back together again; like sometimes you see the man working on the phone lines on the side of the road. It looks like a mess; how can anyone possible connect the right wires together? Somehow they do. But only God can put Matt back together again, and Phil's dream gave us hope that that was exactly what God was doing. God led Phil to this verse for Matt, "And after you have suffered for a little while, the God of all grace, who called you to His eternal glory in Christ, will Himself perfect, confirm, strengthen, and establish you." (I Peter 5:10)

Over the next few days, Matt developed a really high fever. He still had pneumonia so they did a bronchoscopy and cleaned out a lot of mucous. He sat in a recliner for almost an hour. It was so good to see him in a natural position and, when I kissed his cheek his eyelids fluttered. That day, one of the nurses told us that Matt's brain stem was injured, too. Nobody had told us that before. I thought it was really starting to sound impossible. I wrote that day:

"without You it's impossible and we are sunk, but with God all things are possible and there is life."

And, I thought, nothing has really changed. The injuries are the same as they were days ago.

Matt was on the ventilator for a week. Being off the ventilator was a big step and, thank the Lord that whatever happened after that, we would not have to make the decision to terminate life support. I will be eternally grateful.

After just one week, Matt began to get agitated. We were told this is a good thing. It is one of the steps of healing from a TBI (traumatic brain injury). They just didn't know how long this step would last. On this day, my verses for Matt had come from Psalm 22. I was going to be teaching from the Psalms whenever I could start Bible Study again. It was snowing, so we left early to get home. I was pretty upset about everything. I felt the Lord lovingly chastising me (that's the word I used in my journal) and I remember telling Him, "I don't know what to believe!" I knew my prayer needed to change. I knew what I wanted, and I still wanted God's will for Matt, but what would that be? What did *He* want? So I cried out to Him, "I don't know what to believe or what to ask for." Then He told me that he had already shown me. I thought "I have missed it"! Then He told me to just listen. So I asked His forgiveness - He is so good and I thanked Him for His mercy, forgiveness and patience. It was right there in Psalm 22! I wrote in my Bible on 1-10-98 - verses for Matt – Psalm 22:9-10, 14, 19, and 22. This was the verse God gave me: "I will tell of Thy name to my brethren; in the midst of the assembly I will praise Thee." "Matt will talk and he will praise Me in church." I had read those verses to Matt that morning. I had indeed missed what God was trying to tell me, but now I knew and now I would pray. I still praise Him for His faithfulness and patience!!

I still just wanted to hold Matt in my arms and I couldn't, but God provided a substitute. Olivia Hampton (her family were part of our church) was 19 months old and came with a friend from church, Brad and his son, Michael Carlson (for some reason, Brad was babysitting Michael and Olivia that day) to visit with us in the waiting room. She was such a sweet little girl and she climbed up in my lap and let me hold her the whole time they were there. I felt like I was holding Matt. I don't know why or how; but I did. It was a gift from God and Olivia - and I will always be thankful for the gift of a child in my arms that day.

Matt was still in ICU, but they were talking about putting him on the Neurological floor. The nurses were fighting to keep Matt because he still needed the extra care, but the hospital wanted to move him. By day 10, his gut was working, and that was a huge step, but they did not remove the NG tube right away. He was still on warmed oxygen, but breathing on his own. On day 13, he opened his left eye about a quarter of an inch. Praise the Lord!

Chapter Nine

We knew when we left Phil's mom, Maxine, in December, just a few days before the accident, that we probably would not see her again in this world. Phil's brother Steve called about 11:30 Pacific time and told us Maxine had died quietly in her sleep. She went to heaven on Tuesday, January 13th. I wrote at the time, "I can just see her running and dancing now!" She had been in a scooter or bed for many years and had finally been set free.

When we got to the hospital that day we couldn't get in to see Matt. They were putting in a new central line and he was back on an IV and stronger antibiotics. Essentially, nothing had changed. I was just ready for him to wake up. They had warned us from the beginning that this was not like the movies. He was not going to just wake up one day and be like he was before. It would be a process.

I really did not want Phil to go to Georgia for his mom's funeral, but I knew he would and that he should.

It really scared me to think about him not being there with me. Daddy was coming and at least I would not be alone. I was thankful, but it was not the same as Phil being there. He planned to be gone five or six days. Phil left about 6 a.m. and Daddy arrived the same day about 11:30 a.m. They let us back about 1p.m. for daddy to go in and see Matt. He seemed a little more responsive, and, later that day he did open his left eye again - just a tad.

On day 16, I woke up and shared my heart with God. I told him I needed some encouragement that day. When we arrived, Matt's temperature was normal! They put Matt in a chair and he sat straight up for about 45 minutes. His pupils were equal until his time in the chair, but after the chair they did not react together. His eyes looked clear and bright when he opened them. (A miracle day!)

I cannot say enough good things about the nurses in ICU. They were all amazing. They were kind and caring and great nurses and I will always thank God for each one of them.

During the night of the 16th day, Matt was moved to the fifth floor - the Neurological Floor. There were no aids, and there were 3 -5 patients for one RN. His room was right across from the nurse's station. Matt was in a normal room and we could now see him all day. The first night I was lectured by his nurse. She said I was over-stimulating Matt and even said that I should not sing to him. I may have overstimulated him, but I was not doing anything different from what I had done while he was in the trauma unit. (Looking back, to her defense, I think she thought that I had just arrived from Georgia and she needed to instruct me.) The worst part was that she was berating me with Matt lying in his bed between us. I'll just say that was a straw that almost broke my back. I cried all the way home. I called one of the ICU nurses and told her what had happened and what I had been doing. I did want to know if I was doing something that would harm Matt, but I did not want to be told that way. She assured me I had not damaged my son. That night I started a list of things I was thankful for. Looking at it right now, some of it is really hard to read. The Lord took care of everything and that particular nurse was not assigned to Matt again for many days. By that time we were all fine because we were communicating a lot better.

He had great nurses and physical, occupational and speech therapists.

On January 19th, Matt opened both his eyes - the right one just a little and the left more open than I had seen it. (Miracle) He also opened his mouth like he was trying to talk and his legs began to tremble. He relaxed in just a few seconds. He was moving his right arm more than I had seen. The next day I went with Nicole to sign Matt up for Medicaid. The Lord went before us! We had a very nice man who gave us all we needed and the Social Worker at the hospital helped fill out all the papers. She was wonderful too. That day a blood clot was discovered in Matt's right leg. He had a Greenfield filter placed in his Vena Cava to keep any clots from moving up into his lungs or brain. It is still there today.

Dr. Paduch was so happy when we got to the hospital; he had asked Matt to open his eyes and he did! Then, Dr. Van Meter came in and asked the same thing and Matt did it again. Then granddaddy said to him, "It's dinner time. Time to eat!" and that time his left eye opened. It had truly been a good day. Unfortunately, it was time for Daddy to go home the next day. I thank God that he was able to come and be with me. I don't know what I would have done if he hadn't been there.

The Lord was giving me verses during this time and I was sharing most of them with Matt every day, but on February the 2nd He gave me this verse: "Jesus said to her, 'Did I not say to you, if you believe, you will see the glory of God?'" (John 11:14). I wrote the date in my Bible and these words, "Yes, Lord, I believe." Two years later I read this verse and dated it February 2, 2000, and wrote in the margin,

"Lord, God, I trade all my "ifs" (vss. 21 and 32) for Your One "if" (vs 40). Amen."

I was trading all my worries for the glory of God. It had become my prayer that no matter what happened - Jesus would always be glorified in my heart, my thoughts and my actions. Have I always been successful? I'm afraid not, especially in my thoughts, but God has always been faithful. And it is still my prayer.

Because Matt's eyes were not tracking together, they covered his right eye with gauze. He did not like that. That particular treatment did not last long. Matt had his first swallow test, and failed. It took about two hours for the dye to reach his lung mucous. They said that was pretty good. On February 4th, Matt's eyes reacted together when they shined their pin light on one. That was huge. (miracle) He was able to give you an okay sign now, too. Praise the Lord!

Three weeks after the accident, the nurse asked Matt to move his thumb and he did – twice. But he would not do it for the doctor. A response had to be within so many seconds to count. I can't remember what they were now, but he was very slow with all of his responses. We were encouraged because every little step was huge. One day Dr.O'Neill came in and told us that every little step was good and a significant progress could be made between 3 and 6 weeks, and not to let anyone put us down! Praise the Lord!

On day 25, Matt really looked at me and his eyes followed me around the room! The next day he raised his left arm and looked like he was reaching out for something or someone! It was glorious! Matt's left arm was contracting so they put an inflatable cast on it so that he could still move a little. Matt was trying very hard to wake up. He was moving more and more. He was off oxygen but receiving humidified air. Dr. Paduch came in on day 30 and just stood and looked at Matt and said, "He has both eyes open. Amazing!" He said it kind of in awe and I just thought. "Yes, Lord, You and Matt can just keep on amazing them". Nurse Mary Jo told us that Matt is no longer in a coma; he was in an altered state of awareness. I was thanking the Lord; January is finally over!

The more alert Matt got, the worse his muscle tone got. Maybe you, like me, thought that tone was a good thing, right? Not when you have too much of it! His tone was so strong that it was pulling his body toward the left. He began to have foot drop – simply put, he was not able to flex his foot - so they put metal-framed boots, covered with sheepskin, on both his feet. He bent them. That is how very strong he was. They injected his legs with Botox to help his shin muscles relax. It did not work. To stop the contracture in his left arm, the occupational therapist put a cast on his arm and cut the bottom out so you could still exercise his range. It had to be changed about every three days.

Sometimes, I thought I saw fear in Matt's eyes. So I prayed that Matt would sense God's help and presence in ways that I could not imagine, and I would read scripture to him. I wish I could share all the scriptures I read to Matt those days, but there is just not enough room. The serious talk about Matt being moved to a facility began. Of course, by this time, I was just praying that the Lord will provide a good and close place. Day 40 there was another swallow test and he passed the first one. Seven days later, Matt tasted applesauce. Now I thought that I already knew how seriously Matt had been injured, but when he did not know what to do with applesauce in his mouth I really knew. Matt had never had trouble knowing what to do with food.

Matt's body thermostat was all messed up. He was hot all the time, no matter the temperature of the room, so they just kept a pillow case over his lap for modesty. Well, I did not like that very much, so I started making him lap covers. There were patriotic ones, outdoor ones, Nascar, Georgia Bulldogs, Atlanta Falcons, dogs, and other kinds. He looked so much better to me.

Around Valentine's day we received a letter from Kaiser Permanente offering Matt hospitalization. When he was fired the year before, Sealy mattress Co. had failed to offer him Cobra insurance and, by law, they were now offering it. And, if we wanted to pay the back premiums it would be retroactive! (MIRACLE!!!!!!) Phil and I said we would pay it, but the hospital social worker said for us to wait. The hospital was going to receive so much more money from Kaiser than they would from Medicaid that they might pay it themselves. She would check. Well, lo and behold, the hospital paid the back premiums! Matt, a man in an altered state of awareness had become insured! It was going to be so much easier to get Matt placed in a good facility closer to home. God was and is so Good! The news spread all over the place. One lady said she got goosebumps coming into Matt's room. She could feel the presence of God. One of his nurses said that God was at work, that insurance thing was a real miracle. The lady that cleaned his room said she just wanted to peek in the room. She heard about the insurance and God was in this room. Praise the Lord! To God be the glory!

After seven weeks, a man from Pacific Specialties in Vancouver came and assessed Matt. He spoke with us and; my impression was that he did not want to accept Matt, but they would have to because Kaiser had a contract with them. (Miracle!!)

He began getting more and more agitated, which really was a good thing, but hard to experience. Jim Bob was his nurse one night and he told us that Matt was humming. Actually, several of the nurses said that Matt was humming. I hoped it was true; Matt always loved music, but I had only heard him groan. Maybe one person's groaning is another person's humming. (I was talking on the phone the first time I heard Matt make a noise. I was so surprised and excited I dropped the phone in the garbage can in his room!)

Matt's wife, Nicole, was a loving, present and involved wife. She was there every day and we were all pulling together to help Matt and each other. It had been that way since the day of the accident. It seemed that God had healed all the hurt and misunderstanding of the previous year and I was thankful!

February 25; day 55 was the last day at Emanuel Hospital and the first day at Pacific Specialties. God was (and is) still with us.

Chapter Ten

At that time, Pacific Specialties was very highly rated in the state of Washington, but I was advised that we were going to have to be proactive. The CNAs were going to have a lot more than three patients. So I prayed again that our expectations would not be unreasonable and add to the load the care givers were already carrying, but that we would fight for Matt in a way that would glorify Jesus.

Another thing I was learning during this time is that nobody really knew what was going to happen with Matt. Only God knew and the only thing I knew was that someday Matt was going to talk in church! I asked the Lord to help me listen to the doctors and all the experts but to trust Him because He did know and to never lose hope. Again, that was my prayer.

The therapists started working with him immediately; they were great. The physical therapist, Mary, sat him up and he would open his mouth. He would hum for the speech therapist, Barbara. Then, in Occupational therapy, he pushed against Liz's hand on command. He handled it all well at first, but was agitated later. It was a great beginning. Eight weeks after his accident Matt communicated with his left index finger: it meant "yes" if he lifted it.

"Do you like to be called Geraldine?" no movement meant "*no*";

"Do you like to be called Matt?" finger up, *yes*;

"Is your mother here?" *yes*;

"Are you in pain?" *yes*;

"Is your birthday July 10th?" *yes*. I asked him if he wanted me to put lotion on his feet. No movement: that was a "*no*", so I did not.

"Do you love your mom?" When his finger went up, it was one of the most beautiful things I had ever seen.

They stood Matt up on a tilt table. While he was lying flat on this table, they would secure him with straps around his chest, his waist and his legs. Then they would slowly raise him up to a standing position. This was supposed to help everything; his bowels, his heart, his outlook. His blood pressure and pulse stayed safe so he tolerated it pretty well. They did that a couple of times a week. (One time Matt actually went to sleep while he was standing up.) They were all working so hard to help

Matt, and again, I will forever be thankful for them.

During this time, there were a couple of families in the church that were very unhappy about some things within the church. They were very vocal about it to Phil. He was at a very low point and, of course, so was I. So this was the prayer I recorded in my journal.

"Lord, please could You move Matt to the next level? Please? And Father, protect our church, but as bread that is broken, use our lives." "I will wait on You; I will trust You and I will praise You." "Your will - Help us to listen, Help us to obey, Help us to love."

Once again, my heart was strangely lifted.

One of Matt's nurses, Margie, became a nurse because her daughter had experienced a brain injury and she wanted to help others through things like she had gone through. She was convinced Matt could read so she tried an experiment. She wrote "watch" on one card and "spoon" on another. She asked Matt if he could read them and he raised his index finger which meant yes. Once she held a cup in one hand and an apple in another and asked Matt to take the apple. He reached out and took the apple. (Miracle!)

When they put Matt back to bed that day, they discovered that he had pulled his feeding tube out. They did not have another one that would go in so they used a catheter tube and inserted it. Then they sent him to the hospital for an x-ray to make sure it was in the proper place. Nicole called us and wanted us to come to the hospital, so we did. They would not let either of us go back when we arrived. Phil and I sat in the waiting room for a long time until Nicole came out in tears. She said that they weren't doing anything and did not know what to do with Matt, even though they received paperwork with orders for an x-ray. I did not ask, I just went back with her. Matt was sweating profusely and extremely agitated. There were towels there and I started drying him off. By the time I dried his whole body, the towel was soaked and I had to start over. There was only an aid or CNA that came by to take Matt's blood pressure. It was something like 210/110, which is dangerously high. I went out to the waiting room and got Phil. The worse thing was that we didn't see any nurses doing anything. The ones we saw were sitting around. They were probably busy, but we needed help.

Finally, we saw a nurse and she came in and said they were waiting for orders. I'm not a quiet person, especially when I am upset. I said clearly and, so she could hear, (and most people in the ER) that she needed to walk over to the phone and call Dr. Fitzgerald and get the orders they did not seem to have. The orders that Matt was there for an x-ray and by then he probably needed some pain meds. His high blood pressure was certainly not doing any good for his brain injury! She started crying. She did go to the phone and Nicole whispered to me that she was probably calling security, but she was not, she was calling her superior. After that phone call, she did call Dr. Fitzgerald and they sent him right to radiology. The feeding tube was in a good place, thank the Lord! They gave him some pain meds and called for his medical transport. I would like to be able to say with certainty that I apologized to her for making her cry, and I think I did, but I didn't write it down so I can't be totally sure.

That day was the last time that I would see Matt intentionally move his right arm or hand or leg. I do not know what happened that night, but I think his blood pressure caused some damage.

He was still on a lot of medicine for pain and muscle relaxers. One of the nurses discovered that when Matt started moaning, the first thing to do was to open his feeding tube. It would relieve the gas that was in his stomach. He couldn't burp so that really helped, and they were able to reduce his pain meds.

Chapter Eleven

I was leading the music worship every Sunday and, often, we would sing songs that I had sung to Matt that week and I gave a weekly report on his progress. One Sunday we had a visitor, a woman whose name I cannot remember. No one knew her and she was by herself. She told me she had lost her son to a traumatic brain injury. She then told me, "God took my son to heaven, but, he will restore your son to you." She said it with such authority. We never saw her again: Makes a person wonder about angels unaware. (Miracle!)

Phil and I had moved into our new home in the August before Matt's accident. It was a new subdivision, so a lot of people were moving in around the same time. We tried to meet as many new neighbors as we could. When we met one couple, she asked what Phil did for a living. Phil answered that he was a pastor, let's just say, her response was not heartwarming. She did not like Christians! She, Heike, worked at Emanuel Hospital in the Neonatal Department. She had heard about Matt's accident and came over one night to see us. After sharing what had happened and Matt's injuries, she looked at me and said, "Wow, life's just a crap shoot, isn't it?" I did not hesitate and I assured her it was not. "God is in control of everything that is happening right now." Then I told her if I did not have hope in God that I would go to bed and never get out of it. She looked at me like I was a little crazy, but she didn't say a word. Heike and John came to our church for a while then they built a new house and moved away. We thought that we probably would never see them again, but God had other plans. Years later, one Sunday afternoon, she came to our house and asked us, "How do you do it? I watched you through that time. How do you live every day with what happened to your son?" She had a paper in her hand, an obituary. Her brother was a cross-country runner and had dropped dead running in the annual Hood to Coast relay race. She needed help and she wanted what we had! We shared with her that it was our relationship with Jesus that helped us live every day. There is no doubt in our minds and hearts; that day Heike became a follower of Jesus Christ! The joy shining from her face was glorious! Hallelujah! The Lord had shown us exactly what good could come out of the pain we were still living through.

Matt went to church in his new wheelchair by C-Van on April 5th. He could not hold up his head and he slept through the service, but he did pretty well. He was not yet talking. I wrote on April 8th:

"I know, and I don't know when I came to this con-clusion, but my happiness and my abundant life does not depend upon Matt's health. Jesus is sufficient."

On April 9th, I spoke with the speech therapist and she explained why she was not able to work with Matt any longer. She told me that Matt had no gag reflex. Without a gag reflex, you cannot eat because you could aspirate and get pneumonia. She had never seen one reappear this long after an injury. So, after she left, I put my arms around Matt and prayed for our Father to restore his gag reflex so he would be able to talk and eat.

The first year, there were weeks I put over 300 miles on my car. The nursing home was five to six miles from our house and the only places I went were the Nursing home, the church and the grocery store. Phil would get home from his office, we would go see Matt and then we would come home for supper. That was my schedule; see Matt in the morning, go back in the afternoon and Phil and I would go in the evening.

Matt was constantly agitated at this point. Every-thing was so difficult for him. He acted like he wanted to talk, but couldn't. It had to be so frustrating. Once again, sometimes singing was the only thing that would calm him down. So I would sing until he got quiet, but, when I stopped he started moaning again. So I would sing and tiptoe to the door and get softer and softer. Sometimes it worked, but not often enough. So I went to the church and made a tape of all the songs I had been singing to him from the beginning; no music, just my voice. I took a small tape player and I would turn that on and leave when Matt seemed to be asleep. It worked like a charm. His CNAs would even turn it on when I was not there. One of the patients down the hall asked if I would make her a copy of the tape. She said it was very comforting. Of course, I did and I praised the Lord!

On April 17th, fifteen weeks after his accident, Kaiser discontinued his therapy because he was not improving fast enough. I was not giving up on Matt, so I talked to Jerry, the social worker. Matt would still have maintenance therapy by a trained CNA. He was ranged regularly and we would also range his arms and legs. I would go twice a week and help Theone, the CNA, put Matt on the tilt table. It was really helping him, but it felt like we had been deserted. No more other therapies. Once again, I prayed with Matt. The Lord was going to have to accomplish whatever Matt needed. There was no money to hire therapists. It was going to have to be God.

One Sunday morning, I was on my way to see Matt before church, and I heard a sermon on the radio about Simon Peter peacefully sleeping the night before he was supposed to be executed. How could he be so peaceful? Because Jesus had told Peter that he was going to live to be an old man. Peter was not old yet; he was trusting God. It reminded me of what God had put in my mind five years earlier; that if I would not give up, Matt would be all God wanted him to be. With God's help I would wait and trust.

I told my sister about the lack of therapy for Matt and that he did not have a gag reflex. She told me to give Matt little tastes of Diamond Joe Syrup. It was very thick so he shouldn't get choked, and Matt loved Diamond Joe, especially on biscuits. (He did not get any biscuits then.) Well, I didn't ask anybody. I just kept some next to his bed and would give him a little every day.

One day, I reached across Matt's bed and apparently I was too close to his face. He bit me. It hurt, but thankfully he did not hold on like a bull dog. He wasn't able to control his movements so it could have been really bad. Because he would sweat so much, I would keep soft towels between his arms and his chest. One day I reached under his left arm and he clamped his arm down on top of mine and could not relax. I thought he was going to break my arm. I called for help, but no one heard. If you encouraged him to relax it would just make him tighten up more. Finally, he was able to relax and I was able to move my arm. To this day, his left side is still very sensitive, but, twenty years ago, if you touched his arm, it was like his nerves were on the outside of his skin. He would totally tighten up and groan. I did learn that, if you just lightly touched his forearm and asked him to raise his arm, he could do it a few inches. It really helped with dressing him.

Matt received Botox injections in his neck to relax the muscles to keep him from pulling his head down and to the left. That was his natural position at this time. Thankfully, unlike the long muscles in his legs, the Botox worked well in his neck. The treatment would not last forever so the plan was to return in three months for another injection.

By day 100 at Pacific Specialties, Nicole had almost stopped coming to see Matt.

Chapter Twelve

Mama and Daddy came to visit in May and brought Matt's cousin, Michelle, and her son, Brent, to see us. Michelle and Brent were great with Matt and we would go shopping and drop Daddy off just to sit with Matt and watch TV. Later, Matt's cousin, Stephanie, would come, too. Mama and Daddy came at least once a year as long as they could travel. It helped so much for them to come see us.

July 10th was Matt's 25th birthday. My sister had come so we planned to have cake and ice cream, even though Matt couldn't have any. At that time, we were not even sure he knew what was going on. But that day, I stopped and asked the speech therapist to check Matt's swallow. I told her that he was swallowing syrup. She said she would. When I got back to Matt's room she was sitting in front of him with her fingers resting on his throat! She turned to me and said, "He's swallowing, he's really swallowing!!" I said, "Yes, I know." We were both smiling. (Miracle) She had never seen anyone get their swallow back after such a long time. Then she told me that she just came to check him to humor me - that she was a mom and she understood why I was asking. If she had been in my shoes she probably would have asked, too. She was really blown away!

Nicole had filed for divorce so on Tuesday, July 27th a lawyer, Matt's guardian ad litem (appointed by the court) came and read his divorce decree to him. On Friday, July 30th, Phil and I met with a lawyer to start proceedings to be named Matt's legal guardian. One week later, we were given guardian responsibilities for Matt's medical decisions. Being involved with the divorce put us in a very difficult position. Matt needed someone to stand up for him because he could not speak for himself. We truly wished we did not have to be involved, but we were. His divorce was not final until December and we were granted total guardianship shortly after.

Matt had to have a barium swallow test before he could begin to eat anything. On Monday, August 10, 1998, Matt had his test. When we arrived, the technician just looked at us like what are you doing here! But, when Matt swallowed, his attitude toward us changed a little. Then, when there was still some in his throat and Matt cleared it on his own, his attitude totally changed! Again, we heard, "He's really swallowing and even cleared his throat!" Yes, we knew! It was glorious! So Matt could start eating thickened liquids and soft food; yogurt, pudding, mashed potatoes and ice cream. Soon a speech therapist would be coming to help us along this path. It was not long before he was eating everything, pureed, of course. In October, his first solid food that was just mashed a little with a fork was a hot dog. He was on his way!!

As Matt began to improve and be a little more alert, I noticed that he could not look straight at me. If we made eye contact, it would last only a few seconds and his eyes would dart away from my face. I thought to myself, this is like a severe case of autism! His ability to communicate is not there - that part of his brain is disconnected! Then I thought, oh my goodness now I know a little bit about how God feels. My heart hurt. He is constantly loving this world, and communicates with us, but we are not responding! Our eyes dart away away from the One who is caring for us the most. Oh, God has taught me many lessons through Matt!

On Sunday, October 11, we were celebrating Karen and Jimmy's birthdays. Matt was there by way of C-Van. Sitting around the table, Jimmy was telling a funny story he had heard on the radio. Matt started holding up his head, then it would drop down, then he would hold it up again, longer. Then, he started to smile; just a little on his right side, but then his whole mouth broke out in the most beautiful, normal smile. Then he made a noise sort of like a laugh. We all saw him and heard him. This is what I wrote that night: "Praise the Lord! Praise the Lord! What a wonderful day. Our God is an Awesome God!!!

After that, we decided we had to bring Matt home. Maybe, being around us all the time, would help him wake up. Jerry, the Social worker, got everything lined up and, on November 9th, Matt came home. At first, the biggest problem was Matt's bed. It was really a piece of junk and Matt was not comfortable or happy. We had a friend in the church who had a connection with a company that made medical air mattresses and they sold us an air mattress for his bed. That was a great day! He was so much more comfortable. He was fairly easy to care for, except for the fact that he was 6'5" and weighed about 180 pounds at that time. I gave him a bed bath and ranged his arms and legs every day. Therapists came by and worked with him and taught me the things I could do. Friends from church would come over and stay with him to give us a break and that was wonderful. They also found an old handicap van and purchased it for us so we didn't have to depend on C-Van. Matt enjoyed my home cooking, but I think that is all he enjoyed. He did not sleep well at all and, if he was awake, he was agitated, and still sweating profusely. I think he regressed instead of improving. We were not able to get any help through the system to help me so I could get a good night's sleep. In January we took him back to Pacific Specialties for respite care so we both could go to our annual Pastors and Wives retreat. The second we laid him in the bed, he just relaxed. I had not seen him that relaxed since he had been home. So I looked at him and said, "Okay, then, here you will stay." At least we had the van and we could go get him and take him places.

His tone was still bad. His left arm was terribly contracted and his right arm seemed to push downward into the bed. He no longer took the strong pain meds, but they were available if he was in pain. I approached the nurses about getting Matt off of the muscle relaxers. I was praying it would help him be more alert. They agreed. He did become more alert, but the contractions became worse.

At that time, it was obvious to this untrained Mama that Matt's left eye was still not working in unity with his right eye. His eye would always be looking a little above where the right eye was looking - kind of like a strabismus. The pupil was also more dilated than the left one. I wondered how well Matt could really see, but there was no point in putting him through a doctor's visit at this time. (That slowly improved. Today, it is evident only when he does not feel good or he is upset.)

Chapter Thirteen

Eighteen months after the accident, Phil was aggravating Matt and he was getting upset and Phil said well tell me to stop! Matt looked at him and said, "NO!!!!!"

(Miracle) To God be the Glory! The speech therapist came back - and nothing happened; no more words. Matt was more alert, but still very agitated. Some days I could hear him grinding his teeth when I walked in the front door. He broke several mouth guards that the dentist made for him. It was awful. I don't know how he didn't break all his teeth! He hated the mouth guard and I could reason with him to a point; if he would not grind his teeth, he did not have to wear the mouth guard. Sometimes that actually made him quit, for a while. Jesus talks about Hell being a place where there is weeping and gnashing of teeth - I cannot imagine how horrible that will be. Thank you, Jesus, for providing a way of escape! I do not want to go there! I've heard enough gnashing of teeth for a life time, I surely cannot imagine it for eternity!

One Friday night we received a phone call from Kay Cardwell (Mama's first cousin from North Carolina). She and Bennie were driving around the country and they were only three hours from us! We were so excited. They came on a Saturday, spent the night and went to church with us the next morning. They were headed up to Seattle, but stayed and had lunch with us. Matt was there, too. Kay was telling a true story about a skunk they had encountered and we were all laughing - then we heard a sound we had not heard in eighteen months. Matt laughed! Now it sounded a bit like the braying of a donkey, but it was a laugh! And it was beautiful! (Miracle!!)

Over his time at Pacific Specilties, Matt had some wonderful roommates and some terrible ones. One wanted to know if he could have Matt's organs when he died. Then there was the one you could not understand until he cussed you out. Those words were clear as a bell. One very nice man had a lot of extra stuff! He was great! All of his junk was not. Another called himself "an Old Finn!" He was very nice but his visitors were very loud and sometimes they would sing some Old Finnish Hymns! They were awful! The words were something like this, "Jesus is dead and I'm not doing too good, either!" Now, that is an exaggeration, but it's pretty close! It was all I could do to keep Matt from yelling out, "Nooooooo". One man was 99 years old and his wife was 98. They were really sweet people. I whispered to Matt that if his daddy and I live that long, we will be married 81 years!! He laughed.

I felt sorry for those who never had any visitors, and I'll be honest, I was pretty judgmental about their families. Our friend Carol's dad moved into the room with Matt and he was there for several weeks. I was there every day and so was Carol, but we never saw each other. So I decided not to judge anymore. I did not live there, and I did not know who was being visited or who wasn't. Another lesson learned.

My brother John came out to see us in April of 2000. He had not seen Matt since the accident. We had to wait out in the hall because they were getting Matt up into his wheelchair. It was a painful process for him and he was crying out. Johnny was having a hard time listening to Matt and I was praying for my brother. I never knew what was going to greet me when I went into Matt's room. Soon they were done and opened the door for us to go in. I said to him, "I brought you a surprise." He looked up and saw his uncle and gave him a big smile! Hallelujah! He knew his uncle. So I said to him, "You stinker, you never smile at me!" but I was encouraged and happy.

On August 16, 2000, Emma Elizabeth Robinson was born to Karen and Jimmy. Matt didn't know it then, but it was the beginning of a great love between him and his niece. It was also a time of big change. I kept

Emma while Karen and Jimmy were at work. I'm sure I was not with Matt as much as I had been. Anyway, for some reason that he could not explain to us, he did not want to eat, and he started to lose weight. I was the only one who could get him to eat, and that was not always a whole meal. I made sure he ate at least one "meal" a day. He still dropped down to 125 pounds. He was 6'5". He looked like he lived in a concentration camp. I'm going to be transparent with you; I was terrified he was going to die and I was terrified that he would not. My heart was so torn. He was so sad and so agitated all the time. I only confided in one other person, my friend Nancy, and she prayed for me and for Matt. Thankfully, he decided to start eating! I will be forever grateful!

There was always a huge staff turnover at the facility. A lot of the best CNAs usually did not stay very long and the same was true for the nurses. The quality of care was not what it had been in the beginning. I had many discussions with staff and it seemed like everything was a constant battle. But God always had someone that took a special interest in Matt - someone that had our back. (Miracle)

At some point, Matt lost the ability to express "Yes" with his finger. I don't remember when his finger quit working, but it did. (Maybe as his hand contracted.) So I started trying all sorts of things to get him to express yes: blink his eyes, lift his thumb, nod his head, and stick out his tongue. I tried everything I could think of, but he could not or would not do any of them. I was sure if he could express a positive answer it would help him so much, because he had no trouble saying no, but he just could not find a "yes" at least he wouldn't for me.

We had been taking him home and on outings in our van. We took him to the zoo, but he slept the whole time. We took him to the Oregon Coast, but it was so cold and yucky we could not sit out and enjoy the seascape! He finally reached the point that he did not want to go anywhere. So, a family in the church took the van for their parents. We were thankful someone could use it.

Phil sent me home to Georgia for a long weekend with family. It was good for me but, as it turned out, it was very good for all of us. Phil called me and told me Matt had a surprise for me when I got home. He finally told me that Matt could stick out his tongue for "YES!" I was so excited! But would he do it for me when I got home? (I won't keep you in suspense. Yes, he did!) I went into his room and said, "Daddy says that you can stick your tongue out for yes. Is that true?" Well, the response was immediate. He stuck his tongue out and not just a little. He was clearly saying yes! So I decided I would take advantage of this moment and I told him, "Matt, I come to see you every day and you either ignore me, you grind your teeth or you growl at me. It would really help me if you would smile at me when I come to see you. I need a little positive reinforcement here!" He looked at me and gave me a great big smile. That was a great day and a miracle. I had no idea what a huge miracle it was at the time. Matt remembered the next day, and the next, and the next. To this day, it is unusual if he doesn't smile when I walk into his room. And I was correct: his ability to say "yes" helped his whole outlook. This was four and a half years after his accident. Let me remind you: one doctor said Matt would not improve after six months, another said one year and another said two years: they were all wrong.

Since Matt was young he suffered from seasonal allergies. Since his accident he had not had any allergy problems. I thought that was so weird so I asked my allergist and he said that it was not unusual. Apparently, the part of the brain that was telling Matt he was allergic to the pollen had gotten disconnected! And that was a good thing! I praised the Lord! (Even this was a miracle!)

By this time, Matt had no restrictions on his diet. He could eat anything! There were only a few things he did not like: sliced tomatoes, warm tuna, cottage cheese and turnip greens (which he did like before the accident). His favorites were steak, fried chicken, fried pork chops, lasagna, and of course biscuits with Diamond Joe syrup. He was also gaining weight. I don't think his brain could tell him he was full. He would eat as long as you would feed him. But once again, he almost completely stopped eating. This was about three years after the first weight loss incident. Before, if you got the food in his mouth, he would swallow it. Now, he would open his mouth and take the food and spit it out. (Maybe it was a control thing?) I tempted him with candy; if he would eat just this much he could have a piece of candy. Sometimes that worked and sometimes, it did not. He was losing weight again; the pounds were just falling off of him. It was early in December and I decided to have a little talk with him. This is how it went:

"Matt, do you know that if you don't eat, you will die?"

He stuck out his tongue.

"So you are telling me you are ready to die and to be with Jesus?"

He stuck out his tongue.

"Okay. I understand that and if that is what you want, I understand and it is okay with me, but Matt, it's December and if you stop eating now, you will die right at Christmas time, and I don't want to think about your death every Christmas for the rest of my life. So, would you eat for me now and then after Christmas if you don't want to eat, I won't try to make you. Will you do that for me?"

He stuck out his tongue and opened his mouth. He's been eating ever since. God is good. He does give us exactly what we need just when we need it - even words!

I was still fighting battles with the Nursing Home about Matt's care. Many days I would walk into his room and Matt's bed and his clothes would be wet and, of course, he would smell like urine. I had battles from the lack of keeping the schedule to turn Matt so he wouldn't get pressure sores to showers! Sometimes Phil and I would just go in and find the shower chair and the hoyer lift and we would get Matt in the shower so he would be clean. I would help the CNAs when they would clean Matt up or pull him up in the bed. I was a big strong Mama and I was glad I could help them. They were terribly understaffed, but I was getting very tired.

I cannot say that I had totally given up that Matt would talk, but I came very close. I didn't think about it very much, and, if I did, I thought that maybe I had just thought that God had told me Matt would talk. But the Lord led me to teach the Psalms again. As I was doing an overview of the lessons and the chapters that I would use I came again to Psalm 22 and the notes I had written in the margin of my Bible. It was like a light came on and I thought "No, I did hear God speak in His Word to me. Matt is going to talk and praise God in church!" I'm so thankful that God is always faithful. I had read those verses, and the notation, many times, but this time I must have been a smoldering wick because the breath of God lit the fire once again. I did not know when it would happen, but I was *sure* that Matt would talk!

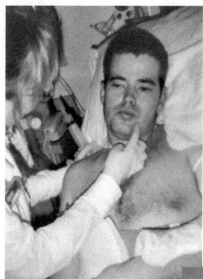

First swallow test

In the Nursing Home on a type
of Standing Table

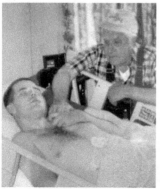

Matt with his Granddaddy

Matt's first smile, October

So thin in the summer of 2000

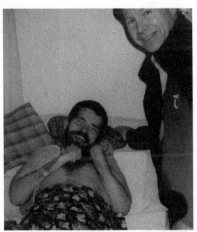

Matt with his Uncle Steve

Jimmy perked him up with a joke

Karen, Matt, and Emma

Grandmama and Jennie, 2002

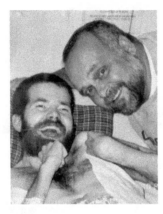

Matt and Johnny

Part Three

"The Lord's loving kindnesses never cease and
His compassions never fail.
They are new every morning:
great is Your faithfulness
therefore I have hope in Him."

Lamentations 3: 22, 23, 24b

"Weeping may last for the night,
but a shout of joy comes in the morning."

Psalm 30:5b

"Finally, my brethren, rejoice in the Lord."

Philippians 3:1

Chapter Fourteen

In late spring of 2004, a large nursing home in Vancouver closed, so those residents needed a place to live. One day they put a third bed in the middle of Matt's room. I went to the Director of Nurses and argued that the room was not big enough for another person - and it wasn't. The beds were probably about four feet from each other and I didn't like it at all. Phil went and expressed his concerns but it did not matter. It was going to happen so we might as well get used to it. In June a relatively young man came and occupied bed #2. His name was Warren Sigafoos. He had been attacked and had a brain injury and was there for rehab. He talked more than any man I have ever met. And he talked to Matt like Matt could talk back to him. After a while, Warren would tell me, "Matt said this or Matt said that." I thought, yeah right. Now, I had heard Matt say "shut up" a couple of times. (There was a man in the room next to Matt's that was a yeller and when Matt had all he could take, he would yell "shut up".) So there were three words in his vocabulary. But I had never heard Matt say any of the words Warren was telling me about.

Saturday, July 24, 2004 (six and one half years after his accident) was a very warm day. Matt was getting very agitated and his fan was on. So we played 20 questions like we usually did when I was trying to figure out what he was upset about. I went all around the room and when I got to "fan" he stuck his tongue out. Then I said to him, "Okay, I'm not playing 20 questions again. What about the fan?" His face got red and he kind of looked like he was revving up his engine and he said, "OFF!!" I said, "WHAAAT?" and he repeated much easier that time, "off". I don't know how many times I asked him to say it. I went to the nurse and said, "Matt just said OFF!" She said I know he's been talking for a couple of weeks. I wanted to wring her neck! I asked her, "Didn't you think I would want to know about that?" She said she was sorry, and how could I stay angry with her! Matt talked! (The miracle had happened!) Hallelujah!!

The next day at church I told everybody that Matt was talking. People were excited with us! Within a week he had said, "I love you, good, Jesus, up, go away, cookie, help, thank you, Emma, Karen, Clifford, and many of the aid's names", and those are just a few. He had not said Mama or Daddy even when I asked him to repeat them. He did say Reese Witherspoon! Now, it took a little bit to figure that one out, but when I did? I said something like, "Okay, boy, if you can say Reese Witherspoon, you can say Mama!!" He looked a little sheepish and said "mama" and then he said "daddy". We did not have that problem again. Kaiser did send a speech therapist in about a week. He was able to repeat everything she said and read everything she wrote. She gave me some exercises for him to do and didn't come back. That was all right, if I couldn't understand him, he would spell it for me; like "Hitlermobile" and "car of death" when he was talking about his car. A month later I wrote in my journal that Matt had a session with PT and he was telling her that Jesus was the reason he was talking. Praise the Lord!!

Even though it was 2004, he thought it was 1997, but he did not remember anything that happened in 1997. He did not remember being married, but he would tell people he dated Nicole for 3½ years. His long term memory was really very good, before 1994, but his short term memory was not working well. He did know who the president was and he could remember things he saw on the news, but every day he asked "what year is it?" and "what day is it?" When I would tell him it was 2004, I could see fear in his eyes. He seriously thought it was 1997 and he was 24 years old; but he knew I was not lying to him. Finally, it hit me that he was afraid that he had lost his mind. So instead of just telling him the year, every time I explained that he was not losing his mind, he had an accident that caused a traumatic brain injury and that was why he could not remember those years. After a while, he accepted it, and it helped. Thank the Lord. The brain is truly a mystery. He could remember jobs he had during that time, but he could not remember his marriage or the trouble he had in 1997. I'm just giving God the credit for that. We had enough to deal with.

As I remembered that time, I only remember the joy! God did what He said He would do! He kept His promise. But as I have read my journals from those days, it was really a stressful time. We were all so excited, but soon Matt went into another depression. He was learning how to live with his condition. He had been in the bed for 6 ½ years. He wore a brief, and like a baby, he dirtied that brief. Well, he did not want to do that anymore. He would ask to go to the bathroom and they would tell him just to mess in his brief. He didn't want to do that! He wanted to go to the bathroom, not use his bed. They did have a shower chair with a hole in the seat so they could have put Matt in that chair, but they did not. He became so unhappy about it, he would try to hold everything and not even go to the bathroom. That created a complete nightmare. He would get severely constipated. That would make him tense up and his legs and back would hurt. The nurse once gave him two Vicodin for his pain - which was caused by constipation which then was made worse by the pain medicine. (The bowel issue was the longest lasting issue. It took a long time, but that finally improved.) I wrote begging the Lord to show me how to help Matt. Now we had a different set of problems and I was stressed.

We reconnected with C-Van, because Matt wanted to go and that was our only option. So I filled out the papers and they wanted a measurement of Matt's wheelchair. Now, measuring his chair, and measuring his chair when he was in it, were two different things. Matt took up a lot of space. While he was still in the hospital, calcium had formed in his left leg above his knee. The PT called it H O, but what it meant was that Matt was growing bone in his muscle even though he was being ranged at least twice a day. The result was that Matt's knee would not bend but a couple of inches. So his three-feet plus long legs stuck straight out. By this time, his femur had grown to his pelvis so he could not bend completely at his hips either. He was a long drink of water! His chair was more of a recliner than a chair. So, I called and asked if they would send someone to measure Matt's chair with him in it. They said they would, and they did. Matt's chair passed the measurement test! Hallelujah!

His primary care physician referred him to a Physiatrist (a physical therapy doctor) to see if there was anything that could be done to release the contractions in his arms and help his frozen knees. I didn't expect anything much from this appointment, but Dr. Satyann listened and his nurse listened. Then the Dr. looked at me and said, "Let's see what we can do for this young man!" Then his nurse said to me, "We're on your side. You are not alone." I started to cry. As far as the medical system was concerned, we had been on our own a long time. So, we got an appointment with a surgeon and the doctor came into the room and asked me why we were there. So I told him. Then he said something like, "He's been like this for years, what's different now and what do you expect me to do?" I told him Matt had just started talking and he wanted to go places. We were there to make sure we covered all the possibilities and that we didn't miss something that could help him. He kind of settled down and asked a few more questions. Then he said that he needed to consult with some other doctors and he would call me when he learned something. He hadn't called in over a week, so I called him. He never returned my call. Once again, it was up to the Lord, and He would get all the credit and glory! (However, we did stay in touch with Dr. Satyann.)

I did take Matt to a Kaiser counselor and he had some practical suggestions for the facility. (I don't remember that any of them were carried out.) He needed time away from the facility so we would go to the Mall and just walk around and get some ice cream. There was a park across the street from the facility, just to change Matt's scenery I would push him around it. A few times we picked Emma up from Pre-school and we would have a picnic in that park. We would bring him home for lunch and a movie. Cliff Blare, who had visited Matt almost every day after his retirement, organized a visitation schedule at church. Many people signed up. It did not last a long time, but it lasted long enough to get Matt through this time. Slowly, Matt started to settle in and accept his condition that he could not change.

Matt really wanted to go to church, but we had a little problem. When we went to the doctor, we used medical transport; but when went to the mall or home, we used C-Van. When we were rolling out the door all the staff would say, "Have a good time, Matt." This is what Matt would say, "I want some whiskey! I'm going to get me some whiskey!" And, sometimes, it was, "I'm gonna get some whiskey and a woman!!!" He also said it in his room sometimes. I wondered what Warren and Matt were talking about when I was not there! I hope you are laughing because it still makes me laugh. I would just shake my head. What was I going to do about that? The therapists at the hospital had warned us that when he started talking he might say things we had never heard before! Well, I promise, I had never heard Matt say those words before! So, when he started saying he wanted to go to church, I decided it was time for a talk. "Matt, I can't take you to church yet."

"Why not?" he asked.

"Because what would we do if you were at church and you yelled out 'I want some whiskey and a woman?'"

He had this horrified look on his face and said, "Mama, I don't know why I say that, I've never liked whiskey!" So we went to church after he promised he would control his tongue. Of course, I could not count on that because Matt couldn't remember what he had promised. But he always behaved himself. He loved going to church and we loved having him there. Everybody loved his laughter.

Chapter Fifteen

On Labor Day weekend the nurse called and said Matt had scabies. They had other cases in the building and the Dr. had ordered medicine for him. Well, I went to see Matt and, when I got there what was on Matt did not look like scabies to me so I declined the medicine and said I wanted the Dr. to see him before he started taking any meds. So the next week, the Dr. agreed, it was not scabies but the sores did not go away. Matt did not itch, so we all reasoned that it couldn't be scabies, but we didn't know what it was. So I asked for an appointment with a dermatologist and that was denied. We kept taking Matt to church and none of us got whatever it was he had. After three months the doctor finally agreed to the referral for the dermatologist. It was scabies. I felt like the scum of the earth mother! But they were not normal scabies; they were Belgian or some other form that was not typical (of course)! He had to take some pills instead rubbing a cream all over his body. The pills worked and all the sores and blisters went away. Of course, he was quarantined for a couple of weeks and couldn't go any-where. I thought that was like shutting the barn door after the horse was out, but we had to obey!

A few weeks later, I received a letter from C-Van stating that they would no longer transport Matt. They had a picture of his feet being a couple of inches from the seat in front of him. They considered this unsafe, so, for his safety, he was Nursing home bound. They also accused me of falsifying his wheel chair measurements, but I reminded them that they measured his chair and approved it. But he still needed to be able to go and have outings and C-Van was our only option at this time. There was no way we could afford medical transport every Sunday or a handicap van.

So I petitioned them for Matt to be transported to church. We were willing to take the risk. So they did not have to worry about being sued. For his mental health he needed a ride to church. They relented and he could ride on Sundays only. Then, I went one step further, and asked for permission for him to ride on Christmas Day and again, they said yes. I think that was a miracle. Thank you, Lord!

In November, 2004, the church was having a Celebration Sunday! Matt was rolled up to the front of the church and thanked God and everyone who had prayed for him! Of course, pictures were taken, but they are so dark you really cannot see well. It was a glorious day! Once again, God had kept his promise! It was almost seven years later, but it was worth the wait! Matt would say he was not a walking miracle, he was a rolling miracle! And he was right! God is good!

The next week Janine Robbins called and told me she was very burdened for Matt and asked what could she do to help? I told her he loves to have company so visits would always be good, but what we really needed was someone to go and ride C-Van with Matt to get to church. (I had been leaving the first service to go and ride with Matt to get to church for the second service and sometimes I barely got there in time. I was in charge of the music and I needed to be there.) She rode with me the next Sunday and started by herself the next week. That was such a help and a blessing to me, and Matt loved her!

Warren Sigafoos (Matt's previous roommate) had been released from the Nursing Home, but had to return after a few months. He was not Matt's roommate anymore, but he would come down and visit with Matt. He was able to move out into an apartment and he started to attend our church. Warren accepted the Lord as his Savior and was a very faithful member of EVCC. How we praised the Lord!!! (Warren passed away about three years ago. I'm so very thankful the Lord put him in that middle bed! Two lives were changed! Maybe even more – (Miracle)

One day, I was sitting in the dining room with Matt waiting for lunch and Matt looked at me and said,

"Mama, you know I wasn't ready to meet Jesus before my accident, but I am now." Glory Hallelujah! Another time he said to me, "Mama, do you know what my baby girl's initials are going to be when I have one?" I said, "No, Matt, what are they going to be. " "GEM: Gina Elizabeth McCoy. She will be my little gem."

Matt truly loved to go to church. I wish I had a dollar for every time he asked, "What day is it?" If it was Monday, he would say, "Six days" or Friday, "Two days". Everything was counted in relation to when he could go to church. He still does that.

On Christmas day, 2004 Matt and I were waiting for the C-Van to come get us and take us home. It was about 40 minutes late. As we were waiting, I looked at Matt and I said, "Matt, I think we need to ask Jesus for a handicap van for you so we won't have to wait for C-Van." Now, it was the best deal in town. Matt was free and it cost his escort $1.00 to ride, but you could not count on what time they were going to pick you up, and we were only allowed to ride on Sundays and Christmas. So that day in the lobby, we asked Jesus for a van for Matt before next Christmas. In October, 2005, the funds were provided for us to buy a used 2005 Dodge Caravan that had been converted into a handicap van! It had a ramp for Matt's entry through the back and two jump seats for the grandkids! It was perfect! Thank the Lord and the person who made this possible!!! We still have it. It has over 130,000 miles, has been in the shop several times, and has broken down twice- only once when Matt was with us. It is God's van and it's working now better than ever. Praise the Lord!

On January 6, 2005 McCoy John Todd Robinson was born; a nephew for Matt to love. It was another joyful day. Praise the Lord! And on August 11, 2006 Wyatt James Robinson was born! He was a real surprise for everybody. We were supposed to have to wait five years between grandchildren! But what a great surprise! Matt had another nephew to love and to love him.

Emma and I took Matt to see the movie, *Chicken Little*. Matt had not been to a movie in close to seven years and I probably had not seen 10 movies in the last ten years. We got all settled in for the movie with popcorn and a coke, and it started with a 5 -10 minute short film about America. It began with the flag flying in the wind in front of a beautiful clear blue sky. Then we flew all over America; cities, The Grand Canyon, the oceans, the mountains. It was really a beautiful film. When it was over, Matt said out loud, "That was a really good movie!!" Everyone in the theater laughed. I have never seen it since. I'm not so sure it wasn't made just for Matt. We could have gone home then, but he really enjoyed the movie. He loved to laugh and he still thoroughly enjoys going to the movies.

One day, I went to pick Matt up to go to the movies and he was not up and ready to go, so I was helping his CNA get him dressed. There was a blister on his stomach. Then I saw another one. I asked the aid if she had noticed that and she said no, but then she disappeared and returned with the RN. A CNA had gone home that week with Chicken Pox. He had never had chicken pox, but that was not from trying. When he was little he tried to get them from his cousins, but he did not. Now he had them. They had to send off a skin specimen to the lab to have it confirmed. I went in to see him the next morning and he was covered! The red rash and blisters were everywhere. He had a headache and some fever, but he did not itch! Aha! He did not itch with scabies either! So, Matt did not itch from his neck down. That is a wonderful thing! How much misery has God saved him from because he does not itch? Sometimes his face itches, but he can rub his face with his left hand and that is the only thing he can do for himself today.

Matt loved the Oregon Coast; especially the Hay-Stack Rocks. (There were three on the Oregon Coast and they stood out not far from the shore like the Rock of Gibralter.) There was a restaurant at Cannon Beach called Moe's. We always tried to be there right when it opened because we took up so much room. The staff was so wonderful! They moved chairs and tables so Matt could be right where he could see the Haystack Rock out in the ocean. We took Matt three times to Moe's; the first time just the three of us, then we took McCoy with us and the last time we took McCoy and Wyatt. He always ordered fish and chips! Matt loved taking those boys to this spot. He always bought them something. The last trip he bought them Shark hats!

The other thing he liked to do was take the kids shopping for their Easter outfits. The four of us would go to the Mall and they got to pick out their outfits. He loved Emma modeling a new dress and the boys choosing their outfits. And they did. McCoy was very particular about what he wore and Wyatt would only want whatever McCoy was getting. It was a blessing for Matt and people were blessed as they watched Matt with his niece and nephews.

Chapter Sixteen

He was constantly getting infections in his elbow and his hands were very difficult to clean because of how tight his fingers were. He basically had a fist instead of a hand. In 2008 an appointment was made to go back to the same surgical office that we had been to earlier, but this time we would see a different doctor. Again, I did not expect anything to come of this appointment. The doctor came in and asked a few questions and started telling me what our options were. Before we left we had an order for surgery. I was kind of in a daze, and I told the nurse what our experience had been at our earlier appointment (when we did not hear back from the doctor). She wanted to know if I remembered the doctor's name. I did not. Then she told Dr. Wyrick. He was not happy about it. (I wondered if they looked back at old records to see who the doctor was.) So Matt was going to have surgery on his right arm and hand.

Before he could have surgery we had to go to an Occupational Therapist. Matt's arm had to be opened up to make sure there was no infection in the crook of his elbow. That took many weeks and I'll save you from the gruesome details, but that was a nightmare. It was so awfully painful, but it worked. On July 15, 2008 Matt had surgery to release the contractures in his right elbow and wrist and his left thumb. I'm sorry to say that I really worried about this surgery. Mostly I was concerned with how Matt would handle the pain. I felt then, and still do, that Matt had a very high pain threshold, but when it reached his limit he was like a five year old, he would just lose control. Even though Matt was once again a sweet boy, he had one word he would yell when he was in extreme pain. Another thing I had never heard him say. (Thankfully, I have not heard him say that word in over six years!)

A lot of people were praying and, needless to say, Matt did great through the surgery. When they brought him up to his room, the nurse gave him something for pain and assured me that I did not need to stay because she would not let Matt suffer. She was as good as her word. When I returned the next morning, Matt was sitting up in his bed having breakfast! When Dr. Wyrick came in to see him, he gave us more details about his surgery and said Matt was doing great. Matt had a drain in his elbow that was still draining a good bit. The doctor said, "I'm really sorry, but he needs to stay another night because we need to watch this drain." Now, we were in a large private room, in the Firstenberg Tower in Vancouver on the seventh floor. Matt had an RN taking care of him and he was across the hall from the nurses' station. He could watch TV without hearing someone else's, and we had a full view of Mt. St. Helens. I said to the doctor, "Can't you figure out a way we could stay here for a month?" We went home the next morning! Oh, Lord, when would I learn that I don't have to worry?

A couple of years later, he had to have surgery again on his wrist, but his right hand is still drawn up to this day. [It was same day surgery and in recovery Matt was in some pain. They gave him pain meds, but the only thing that helped was when I read scripture to him. I read the whole book of Matthew and into Luke. While I read, he was quiet and calm, but if I stopped reading he would moan.] The contracture in Matt's left arm and wrist was pretty severe so Dr. Wyrick asked me if I wanted him to do surgery on that arm, too. I told him no; at least Matt could use that arm to rub his face when it itched. I didn't want to take that away from him.

Matt could also get very upset when his TV didn't work. We got him a 19" flat screen and he loved it. He was so proud of that television. Well, it started acting up and if you turned it off, it might not come back on. He catnapped around the clock so his TV was on 24 hours a day. One day I came in and the CNA , Dawn, followed me into Matt's room. His TV was not working and he was pretty agitated. I pointed the cable remote and pressed the ON button: nothing. I pushed the on button on the side of the TV: nothing. Then I found the TV remote: nothing. I checked that remote for batteries; it was empty and I did not have any batteries to try. So I pointed the remote (with no batteries) at the TV and prayed out loud something like this, "Lord, this is Matt's TV, not mine, if it were mine I wouldn't be asking for this, but Lord it's Matt's and You know how he loves TV, You know it's the only thing he has to do all day. So please Lord, will you please make Matt's TV come on? Please?" I once again pointed the remote at the TV and pressed the button. It came on! (Miracle) Glory, Hallelujah! Thank you Jesus. (Don't you just love it when you pray and tell God all about what's going on when He already knows?) I had to do that once again and the same thing happened. I thought I better not presume on God again so I did buy some batteries after that. It happened again when I was in Portland teaching a Bible study and they called and told me that his TV wasn't working and they had already replaced it. I didn't get to pray for that one so we bought Matt a new and bigger one. He really loved that one even more!!

The Pacific Conference Annual Conference was the end of July every year. We took Matt one Sunday for the picnic and service. There were many that had prayed for him and we knew they would love to see him and many that he would remember. He had a great time. He saw lots of people and they got to talk to him. After the service, Al Hohensee (a friend and pastor) asked Matt if he ever groaned at his daddy's jokes. (Now, Phil could tell a joke and he could tell a story and still can!) Matt looked up at him and said, laughing, "I'm handicapped, not stupid!" and I thought Al was going to hurt himself laughing. We all laughed.

One day I arrived to take Matt out and he was not dressed. So a new CNA came in and she was in a huff. She rushed around grabbing clothes and shoes. I was trying to help her but she just kept repeating like under her breath, "I'm so sorry. I'm so afraid!" Finally, I said to her, "Are you afraid of Matt?" I could not believe that but then she said, "No, I'm afraid of YOU!" "ME? Why are you afraid of me? I'm a nice person." She shook her head and said, "Matt keeps telling me "If Mama ain't happy, ain't nobody happy!" He still says that a lot! It didn't take long for her to get over her fear of me.

Matt got a new roommate. I don't have room to tell you everything about that fiasco. Mr. B was a very large man and his bed was a full size bed. At least now we had only two beds in the room. I was told by the wife of the man across the hall that at night Mr. B tormented Matt with his remote. He would turn up the volume and change the channel and Matt would get upset. The more upset Matt got, the louder the TV got. We tried getting a remote speaker and putting it on Matt's bedside table. Oh, yes, it was great - for about 3 minutes, then Matt just wanted his TV on whatever Mr. B was watching. Everything was fine while I was there, not at night. Then we tried head phones. Matt was in the bed all the time and, since his chin leans to the left, the head phones wouldn't stay in place and Matt could not move his arms to correct them. That didn't work. (Mr. B would not wear headphones.) I prayed for Matt and Mr. B. I talked to Matt. I asked the nurses to talk to Mr. B. That did not work. It got to the point I was regularly being greeted by the nurses about the TV war between them. Finally, one morning I said, "I don't want to hear one more word about this TV problem. I have talked to Matt and I have prayed. I can't fix it. There are empty rooms in this building that one of them can be placed in! That would fix the problem." Oh, they couldn't do that! The problem did not go away, but they didn't say anything more to me about it. Matt still has a problem hearing another TV while he is watching his own.

Of course, Matt remembered all the hymns from his childhood and some of the early choruses. One day "Blessed be Your Name" came on the radio in the van and he started singing along. He knew every word! I was amazed! I said, "Matt, you know every word of that song!" He started telling me that it was written by Michael W. Smith in his Jr. year. I told him, "No, it is a new song written by Matt Redman and the only place you have heard it is at church." We were both amazed! God is so good!

Chapter Seventeen

O ne day Matt was getting frustrated and he said, "Mama, I can't remember anything!!"

I said a quick prayer and I answered, "Yes, you can. You know me and daddy, and grandmama and granddaddy, and Karen and Jimmy."

"But, I've always known them!"

"Okay, do you remember Emma and McCoy and Wyatt?"

"Yes."

"Well, they were born after your accident. Do you remember Jesus?"

"Yes"

"Then you really remember the important things in life." It was my prayer that he would continue to remember the good and uplifting things in life and keep forgetting the rest.

Matt had a couple of sayings that I use to this day. If we were talking about something that could happen but did not seem possible, he would just look at me and say, "One can hope." And when you asked him how he was doing, he would answer, "Great! All things considered!" People were amazed at Matt's attitude. He was a miracle. That great attitude and his joy and peace had come slowly and quietly. There was no big bang or huge event that we can look back on and say "That was the day!" No, it was just a process. God was continually working in him, and us, just his sweet Presence giving us all that abundant life that I had so desperately asked for all those years ago. Sometimes we need to "Be still and know that He is God." I'm so thankful that I journaled. I had forgotten some of these memories.

There was one thing Matt began to obsess about. He would ask me, "Mama, where are we going to live when daddy retires?" Sometimes he would add, "Are we going home to Georgia?" Now, when he first asked that question, we figured we would retire in Vancouver. Karen, Jimmy, Emma, McCoy and Wyatt lived about a mile from us and we could not imagine moving away from them. So when he asked, I would just tell him, "I don't know, Matt. Daddy is not retiring any time soon." He was okay with that, but he kept asking. Now that was not unusual, Matt didn't usually remember what he had already asked so I was not concerned. But he started asking more and more often, so finally, I realized that he was worried about it. So the next time he asked I said, "Matt, I don't know, but wherever we go, you will go with us. We will not move away without you." That seemed to satisfy him and it was easy to say since I really didn't think we were going anywhere.

Then Jimmy was transferred to Houston, Texas, about 2200 miles from us. Jimmy went a few days before the rest and Karen and the kids flew to Houston on Friday, March 9, 2013. That was one of the hardest days of our lives. No longer would the phone ring and I would hear, "Mimi, can I come to your house and can you come get me?" Or "Do y'all want to come over for supper?" Our hearts hurt, but we knew that this was a good move – a God thing! Knowing that helped, but it was still hard. It was hard for Matt, too. He missed them! We flew to Texas on April the 9th. It did not take long to figure out that we could not afford to live in Texas, but Karen was determined that she would find a place for Matt and then we would be able to move there.

That spring, after Matt asked what day and year it was, he started asking me, "What's daddy going to do to me on my 40th birthday?" Then he would laugh. He did it many times. Karen and Jimmy came back in July and we had a big party for Matt. I had an Over-the-Hill bag that his daddy presented to him: glasses, long black socks, reading glasses, prune juice and more. He loved every minute of it. He loved all the people that came to see him and, of course, he loved the cake and ice cream, too. It was a great day.

That Christmas Karen and Jimmy and the kids returned home to Vancouver. We had a full house, but it was great! Matt loved seeing them. Once again, it was hard to tell them goodbye. I felt like Phil and Matt and I were alone. Now, I know we weren't, but it felt like we were. Off and on over the last fifteen years, I had asked God to please take us home to Georgia. I felt like I needed some family close by, so I asked. It did not look like it would ever happen so I just left it with God.

In January of 2014, we were at Newport, OR for a retreat and having breakfast with several other pastors and their wives. Phil was seated next to Gen. Superintendent Brian Eckhardt, I was next to Phil and our friends Pat and Jack O'Neill were seated across from us. I wasn't trying to listen to Phil and Brian, but Jack said to me, "You might want to listen to their conversation." So I did. I couldn't hear everything, but later Phil told me the conversation boiled down to, would we be interested in moving back to Georgia. He thought there would be a church available in August. The details are not important here, but long story short - in April we met with the leadership of GracePointe Church in Fort Valley, Georgia, about 90 miles away from my parents. We visited three facilities for Matt, but the one our hearts were hoping for was The Oaks in Marshallville. It would not be easy to get a room there. By May, we knew we were moving to Georgia!

We couldn't tell anyone yet, but I thought it would be safe to tell Matt. He would not tell anybody because I did not think he would remember. So I decided to tell him if he would promise not to tell anybody. He agreed. Soon after that, as I was walking down the hall to his room, I was stopped by his CNA and asked, "Are you moving?" I froze. Then she said, "Matt says you are moving to Texas." I relaxed. I told her that we were not moving to Texas! That was the truth! The short term memory was improving! I have not told him any more secrets!!

We announced to East Vancouver Community Church on Mother's Day that we were following God's leading to Fort Valley, Georgia. That evening a young couple in the church called and wanted to buy our house. Another adventure had started. Phil informed Spencer Windham at the Oaks Nursing and Personal Care Home in Marshallville, Georgia that we wanted to put Matt's name on the list for a room. He said great, but they had no available rooms at the time.

It was Phil's job to find a way to move Matt across the country and to find the best and most economical way for us to move. He thought about the two of us taking Matt in the van. That idea did not last long. Then he looked into flying Matt across country. You would not believe how expensive that was! He started contacting medical transport companies, and he decided on Eastern Royal Medical Transport out of Atlanta. He found another company to ship Matt's van, but we could not send anything extra in it. When I was told it was going to cost $900.00 to ship Matt's wheelchair, I called and asked if we could secure Matt's wheelchair in his van. They said of course we could. Thank the Lord!

My plan was for us to move and then I would fly back so I could travel across country with Matt; that way he would be in his familiar room with familiar care givers. (Just a few weeks earlier they moved Matt to another room for one night so they could deep clean his room. Matt was not happy! He wanted his room and his TV!) So this plan made sense to me, but God had other plans. On May 15th we got a call from Spencer Windham at The Oaks that they had a room for Matt - now. Phil asked how long they could hold it and he said we needed to start the process now. He really could not hold the room indefinitely. I won't go into all the details, but it was a stressful time. It felt like the Vancouver facility really did not want Matt to go anywhere. They would argue about what they needed to do, and the papers they needed and what we needed to do, but finally everything was faxed to Georgia and received! Even after that there were little things back and forth, but they all got done. It was so stressful! Much prayer and many scriptures brought us through once again.

A date was finally set. Friday, June 6, 2014 (D-Day) at 6 pm PDT the Eastern Royal Medical Transport Company would pick us up. Phil and I would not be leaving for Georgia until the end of July. I was so concerned about leaving Matt alone in a new place. I remember putting my head down on the kitchen cabinet and just weeping out loud, "My son, my son, Lord, help me! Lord, help him!" I don't know how long it lasted, but that battle was won that day! Once again I surrendered Matt into the faithful hands of God.

We were told that we could take some movies - they would have a DVD player. I cannot tell you how badly I dreaded this trip across country, but DVDs would help. I had a team of prayer warriors that I would text as we traveled. My first text was: "we are pulling out of the parking lot now. There is no DVD player! Please pray!!" and they did. Matt did not need a movie! He had the whole country to see and he thoroughly enjoyed it. Riding through the Rockies, seeing the Pronghorn sheep in the plains and even some wild turkeys was wonderful and the weather was perfect. Our drivers were Tony and Jamal and they were great! Matt could have anything he wanted to eat. Jamal would find a steak house if Matt wanted a steak. Matt thought about that one, but decided on McDonalds. (Tony was really disappointed with Matt's choice because they got to eat what we ate.) They drove in four hour shifts. We usually filled up and ate and went to the bathroom all in one stop. Of course, one of the guys was always with Matt; he stayed in the van. Matt had an extra-long bed and I had a recliner seat. It was our prayer to be a good witness for Jesus on this trip. Matt told Jamal all about his missionary nurse Aunt Jennie in Kenya and our time at the mission. Matt was really the good witness. I just filled in some details. We were well into Kentucky before Matt had any pain. Some Tylenol and repositioning took care of that. We pulled into the driveway at the Oaks on Sunday, June 8th at 6 pm EDT (This was within 30 minutes the estimated time they had given Phil). The trip had taken 45 hours. Matt was home.

Chapter Eighteen

Matt settled in at the Oaks right from the start. He had a private room which was an answer to prayer! No more TV wars! I had planned to rent a car since Matt's van would not be there in time, but Sallie Sirmon, a member of GracePointe, had a car I could use. There was a lot to do over the next three days. We had bought a new air mattress for Matt's bed. It had been shipped and it was on Matt's bed, but the pump did not work. So Monday morning Phil had another one shipped, and it arrived the next day. On Monday, I had to go to the Social Security office to transfer Matt from Washington to Georgia - that person was very helpful. On Tuesday I got lost going to Walmart from the Oaks. I didn't know where I was going but I knew my phone GPS was taking me way out of the way. So I called Phil in a panic and asked him to get out the atlas and tell me where I was and how I could get to Perry, GA. He did and I finally got there - a little tense, but safely there. I bought Matt a flat screen TV, a white erase board and a DVD player for his early birthday present.

I was staying with Mrs. Elizabeth Thames another member of GracePointe - a true southern lady that definitely has the gift of hospitality. On Tuesday night, she took me to the Mennonite Restaurant in Montezuma and she invited two ladies from the church, Patty Davis and Ruth Joiner, to go with us. The ladies were a delight and the meal was delicious. We stopped by to see Matt on the way home. I introduced Matt to the ladies and I think the ladies were a little nervous, but Matt put them right at ease. He looked at them and asked, "Do you ladies have any hobbies?" I know my mouth fell open. (I expected Matt to ask them this question - "How tall are you?" because that was what he asked everybody. Then he would say, "I am 6'5". He was very proud of his height.) I had never heard Matt ask anyone about their hobbies! Ruth Joiner spoke right up and answered, "I love to read." They were off and running. They talked all about the Lion, the Witch and the Wardrobe! Matt had a friend for sure." That memory really makes me tear up! It was so sweet and unexpected! Matt enjoyed all the ladies that evening.

On Wednesday my brother John brought Mama and Daddy down to see Matt and to get me. My mother gave me a lecture about how God's timing was always perfect - I had a lot to do and it would probably take all my time just to get ready for our move. Of course, she was right, but I was really all right with leaving Matt. That was settled in the tears on my kitchen cabinet in Vancouver. I knew Matt was right where he was supposed to be. Even Jamal told me, when they were leaving, that the Oaks was a special place and he understood why we chose it - even if it was out in the middle of nowhere. He was right, but God chose the place and opened the door for Matt to be there. And we will always be thankful!

I flew back to Portland on Thursday. The next two months were a whirlwind – packing the house up, packing Phil's office, our General Convention was in Portland and I had responsibilities there, closing out my time as Conference Women's President, good bye dinners, and a party at EVCC. Matt would have been horribly neglected and I would have felt horribly guilty. There were a few trips to the Social Security office in Vancouver before we had done all we needed to do for Matt's transfer to Georgia, but all that was taken care of. Of course, I was calling to check on Matt and every time he was fine! My mother and my brother John - my brother Pat, and his daughters, Michelle and Stephanie came down to visit and check on him before we moved. I was thankful they were close enough to do that.

On July 30th, we packed up a truck and Phil, Rufus, the dog, and I left Vancouver, Washington about 12:30 in the afternoon. There was a big crowd there to help and to see us off. I appreciate every one of them to this day. Tami, Wendy, Sue, and Linda helped with the last minute packing and cleaning. I am forever grateful to them! I won't go into the details of that trip, but we travelled without incident - almost. (There was the time Rufus pooped on my lap and then, the meltdown I had in Kansas City. Other than that, the trip was uneventful.) We had a deal. Phil would drive and I would not sleep so I could make sure he was not only awake, but alert! On Wednesday, August 6th we arrived in Fort Valley! We parked the truck in front of the church and headed to see Matt. We could not wait to see him. He wasn't at all excited that we were there (but he was the next day). Wednesday night service was cancelled that night so they could help us unload and unpack. There were many folks from GracePointe and in a couple of hours everything was unloaded and a lot of boxes were unpacked. Even the beds were assembled and made up. We had a place to lay our heads our first night in Fort Valley. I still thank God for all the good help we had that night, too.

On Sunday the 10th, Phil was installed as the pastor at GracePointe and there was a dinner following church. Matt was welcomed into the church and he loved it. He had not been to church in two months and he was so glad to be there. Soon he was inviting people to church. One day he invited his CNA to come to our church. She asked the name of the church. Matt looked at me and said, "Mama, what's the name of our church?" It took him a while to remember the name, but he always told them his dad was the pastor and he knew they would like it. Then I would give them the pertinent information.

Matt was finally in Georgia and he was happy. I would pick him up one day during the week and bring him home, or we would go to the movie. A few times, we made the trip to Sharpsburg to see his Grandmama and Granddaddy. He loved those trips and he especially loved going to Sprayberry's Barbecue in Newnan! We would go to the newer one because they did not have any steps, and there was plenty of room for him in his chair! Phil's brothers and their wives also came down to see Matt. He hadn't seen Tim for a many years and he really didn't remember that he had seen Steve and Lisa in Vancouver, but he really enjoyed their visits.

Matt really loved going to church – and still does. The church family, children and adults, really made him feel welcome. There were many that would make sure that they stopped and talked with him, not just to say hi, they would visit! At first, I would leave after the music in the first service and go pick Matt up and be back for the second service. When we finished the Children's wing, I started picking Matt up before Sunday School, but he took up so much room he did not fit in any of the adult classes, so I would leave him in the kitchen area and people were always coming and going so he could visit with them. One morning, Liana Walton said to Matt, "Aren't you going to Sunday School?" He just looked at me and I explained that the rooms were too small for Matt. She said, "Well, why don't you come to my class?" (She taught first and second grade.) He looked at me and I asked him if he would like to do that. He did not hesitate, he wanted to go. So that began Matt's ministry with the children at GracePointe.

I started getting reports about how much the kids loved Matt, and I already knew he loved them. Then Julie Beasley told me that her daughter, Adalee, told her something like this, "Mom, I love Mr. Matt! He is so smart. He laughs so much, and He knows all the answers to the questions, and he sings and knows all the words, and he dances... Well, he's dancing in his heart!" (I particularly like that part!) And when she would refer to her class, it was not Mrs. Liana's class, it was Mr. Matt's! She did not want to be promoted to the next class because Mr. Matt would not be there. Sometime after that, Gina Staggs (She and her husband Harvey are our children's pastors) was talking to me about Matt's presence in the children's wing. She said, "Beth, Matt has a real ministry with these kids! They are not afraid of someone in a wheel chair! They know he is a person just like everybody else." And I think seeing him every week in church and Sunday School, in a wheelchair, laughing and singing and enjoying life is also teaching them more than our words ever will. It was later when it struck me – Matt has a ministry – He has a ministry with children! After all these years, God has given Matt this ministry! God had answered our prayers! God was using him in ways we never imagined and certainly in a way that we never dreamed! God is good! He is so good and faithful! Matt's call to ministry was fulfilled at GracePointe in a wheelchair so many years later! Waiting on the Lord may not be easy, but it is always worth it!

I think he also has a ministry at the Oaks. I have had more than one CNA tell me that sometimes if they are having a difficult day, they take the time to stop in and visit with Matt for a minute. He lifts their spirits. That's a ministry. Praise the Lord!

Chapter Nineteen

Kidney Stones! On April 17, 2017, Easter Sunday, Matt was having a wonderful time at church. Sunday School and Church had been a time of rejoicing that Jesus is alive! During the closing song, I looked down at Matt (which I usually do. I love to watch him sing and worship in song!) and he had a horrible expression on his face. He was either sick or in pain. I leaned down and asked what was wrong. He said, "I think I'm going to be sick!"... Some of you already know this, and I don't want to be overly dramatic, but kidney stones are HORRIBLE! Since that day Matt has had numerous attacks. Three surgeries (one was to grind up a dime sized stone in his left kidney and it took four hours!) Six ER visits (one was during a flu epidemic and the last one was during Hurricane Michael and a tornado at the same time!) and four hospital admissions. I have to admit that when we had to go to the ER during the Flu epidemic, I actually thought, but did not say out loud, "What are you thinking, Lord?!" I repented of that almost immediately and I asked God to forgive me, help my sorry attitude and if He could clear the Red Sea, He could clear the ER. I did not deserve it, but He did it! There was not a single soul in the ER waiting room when we arrived. I had learned my lesson, I did not even think that when we had to go during the hurricane-tornado.

One of the horrible things about kidney stones is that they don't give you any warning. With Matt, he could be feeling fine one minute and the next be in horrible pain. That is hard. As I write this, we have not had to make a trip to the ER since the hurricane-tornado. And I hope we don't have to go back. The only thing he can do to help is drink more fluids. Now Matt has to drink thickened liquids and that does not help his liquid intake. (Thickened water taste terrible.) Matt is offered punch every morning and afternoon besides what he has with his meals. Sometimes he says, very politely, "No, thank you." We have learned a little trick that helps: we ask, "Matt, would you rather drink some juice or be catheterized?" He laughs and says, "Punch, please." The last x-rays showed improvement in both kidneys. I don't exactly know what that means, but I'll take improvement and Praise the Lord! (Miracle)

Matt loves for me to read to him and I love to read out loud. We have read many books and stories over the last 22 years. He loves Jan Karon's stories of Mitford and father Tim, Cynthia, Dooley and Barnabus the dog! He loves to hear about Louis L'Amour"s Sacketts and Hopalong Cassidy. His favorite is *The Chronicles of Narnia* by C.S. Lewis. We are just starting our fourth reading of the stories of Narnia. I don't mind. I love them, too. Almost every day we read one chapter of the Bible and then one or two chapters of a book. But one of the best books we have read together is Randy Alcorn's Devotional, *50 Days of Heaven*. As I started reading to Matt, he started commenting, so I wrote down what he said. I want to share these three with you.

Randy – "What will it be like to see true beauty...?"

Matt – "To me, God is going to be true beauty. True beauty will be when I'm standing in the presence of God! To me nothing could be prettier. That's going to be beauty unexplainable!" pg 47

Randy – "You will rise to receive your allotted inheritance' (Daniel 12:13)

Matt – "Oh, yeah! That means I'm gonna be walking next to St. Matthew and ask him what was it like to see a blind man see again! I imagine that in my head: I'm gonna go back and see it all. But to tell the truth, when I get there I'm not gonna care about going back. I'm gonna be happy right where I am!" pg 128

Randy – When we Christians sit in wheelchairs or lie in beds...The strongest and healthiest I've ever felt is only a faint suggestion of what I will experience as a resurrected being...."

Matt – "OOOOOh." With tears in his eyes: "Amen! Great news! I can relate to that!" pg 272

Matt loves music - all kinds - but especially country and contemporary Christian. He loves the music at church. He's the worship team's biggest fan and I know they are blessed by him. We sit right up on the front row and they can see when he gets blessed. One day we were singing a song and the line was "and I'll stand with arms raised and heart abandoned." I looked down at Matt and the only thing he was capable of moving was his left arm and he had it as high as it would go! He was raising his arm in worship to the best of his ability. My heart just melted. I tried to get a picture, but by the time I got my phone out his arm was back down on his chest.

Phil retired in September 2018. Billy Staggs, who had been our youth pastor, took Phil's place and graciously let us stay here. Matt was very concerned about someone beside his dad preaching. He wasn't sure about that at all! But he laughed at one of Pastor Billy's stories the very first Sunday, and has laughed many times since and also had a few tears in his eyes. Pastor Billy has Matt's seal of approval!

Physically, Matt is deteriorating. Every time we have been to the ER it is harder, much harder, to start an IV. He is experiencing more pain in his hips and legs and repositioning him is not really taking care of the pain. So his doctor has prescribed a stronger pain med. Thankfully, and miraculously, his skin is in good condition. His swallow is weaker so now he has to have thickened liquids and there are some things he cannot eat anymore. He can't have fruit like watermelon, he gets choked. He hasn't been able to eat popcorn for a few years, and now he can't have fried pork chops. No matter how small I cut them up, he gets choked. The speech therapist said it is just part of the process. Well, to be honest, I did not want to hear about a process, but that has been surrendered to Jesus, too. Matt can have a sad day but, usually, he is a joyful person. He can have a day when he thinks about what he has lost. But he does not dwell on them. Somehow my son surrenders to God the past and all it holds. He lives with the results of a severe brain injury and his attitude and life glorify God!

Matt loves just being alive! He is very childlike. Matt simply trusts His heavenly Father that He is able and willing to do what is good for him. This is what Matt says about his current condition:

"A lot of people would be mad, but God kept me alive for a reason. I want to do good. I would really like to go the mission field."

I asked him, "Don't you think you are in a mission field?"

"I really don't know. But I smile at people and say hello! And they smile back. At least somebody is smiling for a second."

But, Matt is not afraid of death- he is actually looking forward to it. He has a plan for when he gets there and I quote:

"When I get to heaven, after I finish bowing down for a couple of days to my Wonderful God, I'm going to look for Maxine (Phil's mom) and say 'let's go for a long walk! Hopefully, everybody I know will be there and we can all go for a walk."

Sometimes he tells me he's going to stay at Jesus' feet until he says "Boy, you need to get up, it's someone else's turn!" Matt's not dreading it – at all!

Recently we were reading in Colossians 1:15-20 "And He is the image of the invisible God, the first-born of all creation." These were his remarks;

"To think about Christ becoming a man – for me (he paused). He's thinking about me and He [Christ] said [about me] he might not be able to do much, but he can at least talk about Me. He (Christ) can do the rest of the work Himself. They (the people) just need to listen, and sometimes that's all you need – at least a person willing to talk and a person willing to listen."

We are currently in the middle of a quarantine because of the Corona Virus. He cannot go to church (He got very upset on Easter when he couldn't go to church until the nurse explained we weren't having church.) He cannot come home for a day with us. We can't even go see him now. We had a successful Zoom "visit" this morning. He is doing great. We laughed and reminisced and read a few verses and his daddy prayed. (Window visits resumed after three weeks.) God is able! Someone asked me if Matt would miss us during this time. He probably does in a way, but Matt has no real concept of time like that. His short term memory loss may drive me a little crazy sometimes, but I learned a long time ago that it is a gift from God. Especially when you consider what Matt does remember every day: He is loved and he loves. All those years ago when he remembered to stick out his tongue for "yes" and to smile when I came to see him, that was God! We had no idea what a huge miracle that was. So we have learned to be thankful for what he remembers and leave the rest to God. Someone asked me once why I went to see Matt every day and why would I take him to the movie since he couldn't remember it! I told them, "His soul remembers." And I believe that; his soul remembers every kind and good thing that has happened and all the bad stuff is forgotten! He does not hold a grudge about anything! He doesn't even have to fight it! God is good.

At the beginning of this journey, I never asked God "why". I knew God was at work, but since then, there were a few times I asked God, "Why is Matt still here? If it's not Your will to heal him, why does he have to suffer like this?" I don't think God is upset when we ask why. First, if we are willing to listen and accept His answer and, second, if we are willing to let go of the question if He does not give us an answer. We won't always know the purpose of God; and, the older I get, the less I need to know. It is enough to know that He is intimately involved in every part of my life and I can trust Him. Phil and I have talked about God's purpose in all of this. Paul tells us in Romans 2:4 that the kindness of God leads many to repentance. We believe that Matt is experiencing the kindness of God. Matt did not handle complete freedom very well and God knows that better than we do. The accident brought repentance into Matt's life and surrender to the life God has for him today. Today, he is in God's protective custody and being used all the time in God's amazing plan. He is all that God wants him to be!

Only God knows what the future holds. I honestly do not want to know. I think over the last 22 years, and there have been some difficult ones. I wouldn't change them. It would be nice if we could become all that God wants us to be through easy times, and I am convinced that God will be as gentle with us as we let Him. But He loves us too much to leave us as we are and it takes trials and ordeals to conform us into the image of His Son. I would not take back my prayer for God to do whatever it takes.... He knows what He is doing. Would Matt say it has been worth it? Oh, yeah!

Matt has settled in so well. He is so happy. We are still amazed at his attitude! We had known at the beginning that the Oaks was a good place - a special place. The owners; the Windhams, are on site (in hurricanes and tornadoes and pandemics) and they care! The staff is loving and efficient. They are one of the reasons Matt can have the attitude that he has, but there is another - one that goes beyond outside circumstances or influences. One day Phil asked him, "Matt, you lay in the bed all day and you watch TV. How do you have such a good attitude? Where does it come from?" Listen to his answer!

"Daddy, every morning I wake up and I think that I can be bitter, or I can have joy; so I choose joy. I don't think it would make Jesus happy if I'm bitter."

Just that quietly, that simply – Matt chooses joy! Thank you, Jesus! Sometimes I am overcome with gratitude. Today, life could be like it was for the first 4 ½ years after his accident, or the years before it, when he was heading far from God - years filled with frustration and anger and fear - but it is not! Abundant life is ours! Matt chooses joy every day. What an impact that has made on my life. If Matt, 100% handicapped and lying in a bed can choose joy, so will I!

And his story is not over yet!

Epilogue

I have been questioned about my statement that you can choose joy. Apparently, some people don't think that is possible, but I have watched Matt choose joy for many years. Let me say that I don't believe that you can conjure up joy, but I know that in the Scriptures, God tells us to rejoice – many times. I believe that God does not tell us to do something that He won't help us accomplish. Hopefully, I have made this clear in the book, I believe that if we want to choose joy, there are some conditions that have to exist. I would like to share some scriptural conditions with you.

It is impossible to have true joy outside of a relationship with the Lord Jesus Christ. If you don't have a relationship with Him, please consider what I am about to share, and if you do, consider anew the wonder of what God has done.

- In the beginning, God created the heavens and the earth and the first man and woman, and He declared that it was very good – perfect. God and mankind had a perfect Father and child relationship.

- At some point Adam and Eve were tempted by the serpent and they disobeyed God and ate the fruit that had been forbidden.

- Sin and death entered God's beautiful creation and the earth and all who live on it were cursed. But God made a promise that one day the seed of Eve would crush the head of the serpent. *Genesis 1-3*

- The earth became more and more wicked and God sent Moses to lead the people out of slavery and give them the Law – rules to live by. The law provided forgiveness of sin through the sacrifice of certain unblemished and perfect animals, but the law could not cleanse the human heart. So the law was given to show us our need for a Savior. *Exodus*

- The four Gospels tell us that at the right time, the Word became flesh and God sent His Son, Jesus Christ, born of a woman to live among us. He lived a perfect and sinless life. He healed people, He cast out demons, He raised people from the dead. He taught about the Kingdom of God and so much more. As He went about and taught, He invited people to "Come" and follow Him. According to the scriptures He came to restore what the devil had broken –

a relationship with God. Then He died on a cross and shed His blood to be the perfect sacrifice for our sins, once and for all. Three days later He rose from the dead!

- According to the scriptures we are all sinners and need a Savior. *Romans 3:23*

- According to the scriptures we cannot earn salvation or deserve it or work for it, or follow enough rules; it is the free gift of God. *Romans 6:23*
- According to the scriptures Jesus is the only Way to God the Father. *John 14:6*

- According to the scriptures He is coming back and we are to be faithful laborers until He comes. *Matthew 24:51*

- According to thescriptures God gives us unique gifts that enable us to do good works that He planned for us long ago. We are His workmanship. *Ephesians 2:10*

- Jesus invites all of us to come and follow Him. *Matthew 11:28*

- According to the scriptures, any who receive Him become children of God. *John 1:12*

- According to the scriptures, if we are a child of God when we die we will spend eternity in Heaven with the Lord. *John 3:16*

- According to the scriptures, there is nothing that compares with knowing Jesus. *Philippians 3:7-11*

If you know Jesus Christ and are following Him, Rejoice! If you don't know Him, search the scriptures, pray and ask Jesus to forgive your sins and make you His child. Seek Him with all your heart. He is calling.

The next condition is surrender. After we know Jesus we have the ability to surrender our lives to Him. You don't find the word "surrender" in scripture but a few times, but you certainly see the principle. Jesus tells us to take up our cross and follow Him. I believe that taking up our cross is an act of surrender. We are laying down our own dreams and perceived needs and wants so we can follow Him and when we do that we also learn we can trust Him. When we trust Him we have peace and when we have peace we have joy. I heard a retreat speaker say, "We can have joy and be sad at the same time." I believe it. I have experienced that and I think Jesus did. And I am pretty sure Matt has, too.

I just want to add one more thing. We need to be thankful. A relationship with Jesus and surrendering to the loving arms of God with a grateful heart – this is the only path to true joy.

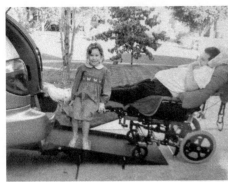

Matt and Emma and
his new van

Matt, choosing joy

Haystack Rock at Lincoln
City with McCoy

Matt, McCoy, and Wyatt, on the Oregon coast in their shark hats

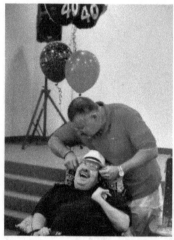

Matt's 40th birthday, receiving his Old Timer's kit

Family picture on Matt's birthday

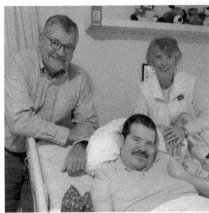

Christmas 2019

The door to Matt's room at The Oaks

Some of the kids from Sunday School, with Adalee laying her head on Matt's chest

Preparing for surgery

Matt, in his own backyard.

Every Sunday morning, when we pull up behind the church, Matt says, "I love that sign."

RESERVED
FOR
MATT
McCOY

This picture was taken the day before quarantine began. We had no idea we would not be allowed back the next day.

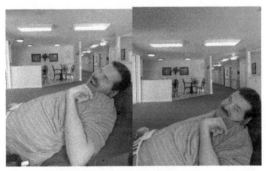

Matt on his birthday

Acknowledgements

This story and this book would have never happened if it weren't for the prayer warriors and encouragers we have had all along the way. To all the people that have prayed for us, even if only once, we are forever grateful. We've also always had the support from a great family; the ones we were born to and the family of God!

To my family, and friends from the Southeast to the Pacific Northwest and places in between who prayed for me during the writing of this story – I couldn't have done it without each of you. When I wanted to give up, you were encouraging and praying. Thank you so much.

I would love to make a list of names here, but for fear of leaving someone out and to be honest, I only remember faces in some cases; let me just say that we have experienced love and care from many nurses, therapists, nursing assistants, doctors, and the entire staff at The Oaks. I cannot thank them enough. God has always had someone that loved Matt and cared for us all. Thank you! Thank you!

When I put out the request for prayer with the worship leaders at GracePointe, I got support from everyone, but Kaitlyn Staggs and Julie Beasley immediately volunteered to edit my manuscript. I immediately said thank you! Thank you for taking the time to undertake this job! Your corrections and suggestions were great! (Kaitlyn had been an editor before and Julie is a grammar fanatic.) They both were great encouragers.

I want to give a special thank you to my cousin, Beth Middleton. When I was struggling, she encouraged me to put some scripture verses where I could see them while I was writing. There are still four scriptures on the wall in front of my computer that I looked at often. Thank you, Beth. Also her husband, Jeff, who gave me Mark Wyatt's name.

I want to thank Mark Wyatt of Wyatt House Publishing. As soon as I signed with Mark, I felt a weight had been lifted off my shoulders. He has been so patient with me in my inexperience with any of this and with my electronically challenged brain! He assured me he would take care of everything and he has! Thank you so much, Mark!

For fifty-one years I have been so blessed with a husband that has always loved me, encouraged me and believed in me, covered me in prayer, patient in the middle of my angst over a speaking engagement (and any ministry I was involved in), and during the writing of this book he has remained faithful. He was always ready when I would ask, "Phil, what is that word when you …..?" With the hint of a smile he always had the word I was looking for! When I finally let him read the finished manuscript, he continued to encourage me. Thank you, thank you, Phil. I love you with all my heart.

And last but most definitely not least – I want to thank God. He has so richly blessed me in so many ways! He has helped with every step of the writing of Matt's story. His presence and peace is worth more than gold, His help and guidance and patience is greater than silver and his joy is greater than diamonds! His Word is truly a light that has always illuminated my path and that has made all the difference! Thank you, Father! Thank you, Lord Jesus! Thank you, Holy Spirit!

You have a story.
We want to publish it.

Everyone has as a story to tell. It might be about something you know how to do, or what has happened in your life, or it may be a thrilling, or romantic, or intriguing, or heart-warming, or suspenseful story, starring a cast of characters that have been swimming around in your imagination.

And at Wyatt House Publishing, we can get your story onto the pages of a book just like the one you are holding in your hand. With professional interior design and a custom, professionally designed cover built just for you from the start, you can finally see your dream of being an author become reality. Then, you will see your book listed with retailers all over the world as people are able to buy your book from wherever they are and have it delivered to their home or their e-reader.

So what are you waiting for? This is your time.

visit us at

www.wyattpublishing.com

for details on how to get started becoming a
published author right away.

CPSIA information can be obtained
at www.ICGtesting.com
Printed in the USA
FSHW010857050421
80142FS

9 781734 539868